SMILE A WHILE

Previous Anthologies by the same Author:

'What Can I Give Him?'
'Give My Heart?'
'God Who Made The Earth'
'Trusting My Master'
'As I Look Back'
'The Wonder Of You'
'A Child Of God'
'God Has Made All Things Well'
'Love Came Down At Christmas'
'A Very Special Friend'
'Keep Smiling Through'

Cover Photograph 'Honey'

SMILE A WHILE

John Christopher

Date of Publication:
October 2000

Published by:
Highway Books Ltd
49 Common Road

Esher
Surrey
KT10 0HU

© Copyright 2000 John Christopher

Printed by:
ProPrint
Riverside Cottage
Great North Road
Stibbington
Peterborough PE8 6LR

ISBN: 1 901004 11 2

FOREWORD

I hadn't originally intended to put together a second collection of humorous verse, but I was reminded of the importance of laughter when speaking at church recently. One dear lady came up to me afterwards and said 'I would like a book of poetry to cheer up a sick friend'. Somebody who was just feeling low, and in need of a little tonic. We all indeed have times in our lives when we are burdened by either sickness or sadness, and it is at those times perhaps that a smile is needed the most.

So this second anthology was prompted by that and other comments I have received. It is a light hearted look, yes at church life, but also many others aspects of day to day living.

It seems appropriate now to thank those dear folk who have given me such encouragement to write over these last few years. I am certain that without the encouragement I would have laid down my pen a good while ago! Bless you, each one of you. To Norma, who suggested the title of this book, a very special 'Thank You'.

Please enjoy this book. It is my sincerest wish that as you pick it up and look through its pages, you will indeed find that you 'Smile a While'. Oh, and just one last thing. Don't keep smiles to yourself. Share them with a friend, and you will be amazed at the difference they can make!

John Christopher

THE LION AND THE ELEPHANT

The lion felt so fit and healthy, that
he gave a special growl,
then very proudly through the jungle
he went off for a prowl.

'Who is the king of the jungle?'
he asked a snake that he met.
'You are of course!' the snake replied.
The Lion said 'Don't you forget!'

'Who is the king of the jungle?'
he asked a crocodile.
The crocodile said 'Why, you are',
and the lion gave him a smile.

So one by one they all agreed
and said he was brave and strong.
Life was quite good, that was until
the elephant came along!

'Who is the king of the jungle?'
the lion asked once again.
The elephant just stared at him,
then made things very plain!

He picked the lion up with his trunk
and waved him all around,
then when he'd taught the lion a lesson
he dropped him on the ground!

'All right, all right', groaned the battered lion,
nursing a very sore toe.
'There's no need to get angry, just
because you do not know!'

CHILDREN SAY THE FUNNIEST THINGS!

Christmas was coming, and one junior class
performed their Nativity play.
The teacher was keen that her children
should think of their own words to say.

The parents encouraged the children
and the play went quite well from the start.
Then the time came for the shepherds
to come on and act their small part.

The first two were nervous, and knelt quietly down
but quite boldly, the third shepherd lad
looked in the manger, then said to Mary
  'Isn't he like his dad?!'

The lightning flashed one stormy night.
She wondered 'Is my child all right?'
Sat up in bed, he made her laugh,
saying 'God took my photograph!'

  'Where was king Solomon's temple?'
she asked, and Jimmy said
  'Why teacher, that's an easy one.
At one side of his head.

  'Now make up a sentence with beans in'.
  'My father grows beans' one child said.
..'My mother cooks beans' said Sarah.
  'We are all human beans' replied Fred!

The ruler of Russia was called the Tsar,
and his wife was the Tsarina.
Now what were all their children called?'
  'Sardines' replied Georgina!

LOVELINES!

A lady who talked for hours and hours
once paid the doctor a call.
She chatted away endlessly to him,
while the doctor did not speak at all!

'So you see' at last she concluded,
'I speak to my husband each day,
but he never seems to be listening
to anything that I say!'

'I wouldn't have come in this evening,
but it worries me quite a lot.
I wondered if you could tell me if
it's a affliction that he's got?'

The doctor smiled rather knowingly!
He replied 'I have got the drift.
I don't think he has an affliction.
It's more like a very rare gift!'

A husband told his wife one day
  'I've got a good idea.'
His wife replied sarcastically
  'Beginners luck, it's clear!'

The festive season was coming
and so he asked his wife Pat
  'What am I getting for Christmas?'
She said 'Very bald and fat!'

'My wife is certainly rather large!
I have to get out of bed
to see if it is daylight yet!'
her unkind husband said!'

CHURCH CHUCKLES!

Daniel the monk had never preached,
but then came his first day -
He stood up very nervously,
not knowing what to say.

'Do you know what I'm going to preach?'
he asked the people there.
'No' they replied. He said 'Neither do I'
and sat down in despair!

The next week many people came
to hear his short address.
'Do you know what I'm going to preach?'
This time they called out 'Yes!'

'I needn't tell you then' he said,
and he sat down once more.
Next week there were more people there
than had ever come before!

'Do you know what I'm going to preach?'
Half said 'Yes' and half said 'No.'
'Well, will those who said 'Yes' please tell
the others before you go?!'

Two boys were passing the vicarage
when they heard the vicar shout.
'Does this ball happen to belong
to one of you?' he called out.

'Did it do any damage?' Jimmy asked.
The vicar said 'No, none at all.'
Young Jimmy beamed, and then he replied
'Yes vicar, that is my ball!'

LIFE'S LIKE THAT!

A woodpecker spoke to a chicken.
'We are much cleverer than you!'
The chicken was quite clearly upset
and replied 'That just isn't true!'

He said 'I've often watched you, my friend,
and your day it seems to me
consists of banging your head for hours
and hours against a tree!'

'That may be true' the woodpecker said.
'I do that most of the day,
but no one hears of Kentucky Fried Woodpecker,
sold at a takeaway!'

'Have you something to make me sweat?'
the doctor was asked by young Nick.
He said 'I'm going to sign you off.
I think that should do the trick!'

'I feel like a piece of a jigsaw,'
said the worried young man.
The doctor said 'Just wait there.
I'll fit you in when I can!'

She told her daughter 'I'm really worried
about this much older rich man!
You know I want to see you happy
in every way I can.'

'I'm sure that things will all work out.'
she replied contentedly.
'I know that he's got a very strong will,
and it's all made out to me!'

CHILDREN SAY THE FUNNIEST THINGS!

The vicar speaking on honesty
said 'Children, I'm asking you
if I was in the street, and dropped
ten pounds, what would you do?'

Of course young Jimmy, keen to show
that he was free from sin,
said 'I would pick it up, vicar,
and put it in a bin!'

A little girl's father was going to sea.
She asked God as he went away
  'Please watch over my Daddy, dear Lord,
and keep him from danger, I pray'

Then she added 'I nearly forgot.
There's just one more job for you.
While my Daddy's away please will You
keep an eye on Mummy, too?!'

Two little girls were chatting
when sent to play outdoors.
Young Susan said 'My mother
is much nicer than yours!'

Young Sarah said 'my father's
the nicest of the two.'
Said Susan 'If you want to know,
my mother agrees with you!'

Young Jimmy told his mum 'I wish
I'd lived long long ago,
because there wouldn't be so much
history for me to know!'

CHURCH CHUCKLES!

Two men were discussing religion.
The first said 'I'll have nothing to do
with anything that I don't understand,
and now my friend, how about you?'

'Have you had your breakfast this morning?'
The first man then answered 'Well, yes,
but what that's got to do with religion
is really just anyone's guess!'

'Did you have toast spread with butter?'
'Yes I did' the first man agreed.
'Well, just think of a black and white cow
eating lots of green grass for its feed.'

'How can all that turn into white milk
that makes yellow butter? Just explain!
If you can't, I wouldn't have anything
to do with breakfast again!'

The vicar said to one of his flock
    'I pray for you every night.'
The lady replied 'I'm on the phone,
or it's the third house on the right!'

The vicar said to his young son
    'I really do despair!
I think that Satan told you
to pull your sister's hair!'

'Perhaps that's true' his son replied,
    'but it was my idea
to kick her on the keen as well,
and shout loudly in her ear!'

COFFEE BREAK

The music teacher unfortunately
just couldn't control her class.
The English mistress suffered most,
as her room was closest, alas!

One day it was worse than usual,
and sounds echoed through her door!
She hurried into the music room
because she could take no more!

She found the music teacher there,
surrounded by screaming boys!
  'Do you know we cannot hear ourselves
because of all the noise?!'

  'No,' the music teacher replied,
  'but if you could hum the tune
I'll try to follow, and I'm sure
we'll pick it up quite soon.'

Her husband said 'I made a fool
of myself, at that party, I fear!'
His wife replied 'I didn't notice
anything unusual, dear!'

They'd not seen each other for quite a while
until they met up one day.
The first one said 'Dorothy, it must
be seven years, if it's a day!'

  'You certainly look a lot older!'
said she, not one to impress!
Her friend said 'I wouldn't have recognised you,
except for the hat and dress!'

CHILDREN SAY THE FUNNIEST THINGS

'My uncle's got a wooden leg.'
Young Jimmy, not impressed
said 'That's nothing, for my auntie
has got a wooden chest!'

Jimmy said his aunt and uncle hadn't
argued for ten years or more,
then he told me that his uncle
had been living in Singapore!

Jimmy said 'I'll join the army.'
His mother said 'Wait and see.
Right now you're just an infant.'
  'Then I'll join the infantry!'

I said to young Jimmy 'Eskimos eat
raw fish and blubber, they say.'
Jimmy replied 'well you'd blubber too,
if you had to eat raw fish each day!'

'I'd like a day to pass without
telling you off!' teacher sighed.
'You have my full permission, sir'
cheeky young Jimmy replied!

'We're not selling bananas any longer'
the shop told young Jimmy today.
Jimmy replied 'I'm not bothered.
They're all long enough, anyway!'

The teacher said 'Please name ten animals?'
Young Jimmy, prepared for a laugh
called out 'I know miss, that's easy.
Nine elephants and a giraffe!'

SPORTING STORIES!

He'd had his golf clubs stolen,
and the poor man looked so down.
He told me they'd been taken
from the car park in the town.

I asked 'Was your car damaged?'
He said 'I cannot tell,'
Then told me as an afterthought
  'They've taken that as well!'

'Lord, if there's cricket in Heaven'
a cricketer's wife said 'I pray
there is a really good chance that
there'll be some rain every day!'

'I've got a set of golf clubs for my husband.'
Her friend said 'My, you're really doing fine!
I've asked around, and advertised for ages
but can't get anything at all for mine!'

The vicar once in a cricket match,
on the boundary made a splendid catch.
The batsman said 'With his hands in prayer
he's got God helping him up there!'

An angler proudly told his friend
  'I went fly-fishing yesterday!'
  'I caught a two pound bluebottle'
the man was heard to say!

  'Why do you look at your watch?'
a golfer asked his caddy one day.
  'It's not a watch, it's a compass.
It's useful for finding the way!'

CHURCH CHUCKLES!

A bishop once visiting a parish
was invited to afternoon tea.
A rather determined young lady
was eager for his company.

She wanted to seek his opinion
and said to him 'What awful news!
I mean the ship that collided
while on a holiday cruise.

'Now bishop, an Aunt of mine booked
on that trip, I've only just found.
She cancelled, but if she had not
my Aunt may well have been drowned!'

'Do you believe as a bishop
that all these events have been planned,
and that my Aunt was delivered
through the providence of God's hand?'

The bishop was always quite careful
to give very little away,
so replied 'As I don't know your Aunt
I'm really not able to say!'

The vicar had been in hospital
so the curate gave the address.
'I'm sure' he said 'you'll be pleased to know
that he's making slow progress!'

Susan came home from church one day
looking fed up and glum.
'What did the vicar preach about?'
'He didn't tell us, mum!'

ANIMAL ANTICS

A man dashed into a police station,
and cried, in a terrible state
  'Please can you help me at once, as
my wife has been missing since eight!'

  'I need to take some particulars, Sir,'
He said 'What is there to tell?
She is medium height and medium build,
and ordinary looking as well.'

  'Don't worry too much,' the constable said.
  'I can see you are very distressed.
I'm wondering if you can tell me
how is your missing wife dressed?'

He replied 'I really can't tell you,
but our dog is with her, you know.
Brindle, Bull terrier, weights 50 pounds,
and four dark blotches that show.'

  'He has three white legs, and the other one
is brindled, all but the toes.
He has a small nick in his left ear, and
a tiny bald patch near his nose.'

  'Just leave it with us,' the constable said.
  'It's all written here in my log.
It is possible that we won't find the dog!'

  'I took my dog to the vet, because
it bit my wife' he said.
  'Was it put down?' He said 'Oh. no.
I had them sharpened instead!'

LIFE'S LIKE THAT!

He said 'I learned to swim at an early age.
I think I was only three.
I got in a boat with my parents,
and they rowed me out to sea.'

'Quite often they'd take the boat out
about a mile or more,
and then I got out and swam back
until I reached the shore.'

'I thought it was quite a lot of fun,
and didn't mind swimming back,
but I used to have quite a lot of trouble
getting out of the sack!'

'Yesterday I felt like a bell tent,
and today, just like a marquee!'
The doctor said 'You have a problem.
You're too tense, it seems to me!'

The doctor sent me to the chemist,
but I didn't feel quite as fine,
when I saw ;We dispense with accuracy'
outside the shop on a sign!

The supermarket was very large.
Unfortunately, young Sue
got separated from her mother,
but she knew what to do!

'Excuse me,' said the little girl
to the first person she could see.
'Have you seen a mother pushing a trolley
without a girl like me?!'

THE JOYS OF TURKEY!

As we're nearing the festive season now
I shall put an appropriate word in,
and I'll give out my usual reminder
  'My darling, will you get the bird in?'

Our Sarah keeps telling the family
that we're such absolute barbarians!
She threatens that she will disown us, unless
we decide to become vegetarians!

This year I am certain, the turkey
is decidedly plumper and rounder
than any we've had. My wife said proudly
  'It must be a twenty pounder!'

I told her,' Prime Minister's may have
days when they don't need to govern,
but I reckon they won't have a bigger bird
than ours, sitting now in their oven!'

Our turkey is in, and the kitchen has got
a wonderful smell while it's cooking.
I cannot resist just the tiniest peep.
Well, surely there's no harm in looking!

The table is laid, and the turkey's brought in,
and the vegetable sizzle in dishes.
My plate is filled up with the loveliest fare,
and I taste, and pronounce it 'delicious!'

That was six days ago, and I want you to know
that the turkey is getting quite boring!
Our Sarah's left home, and now even the dog
is sleeping each day, and not gnawing!

My wife is the most inventive of souls,
yet even she is undoubtedly worried.
  'We've had mince and rissoles and fritters' she
                                     said.
''This evening, we'll both have it curried!'

That did it! I've decided that I've had enough,
and I've gone off roast turkey forever.
We'll get Sarah back, and tell her that next year
we'll be having nut cutlets together!

COFFEE BREAK

The electrician turned up very late.
The man said 'My, you're slow.
I asked you to mend my doorbell
at least three days ago!'

The electrician said 'I did come round
and rang without reply.
When you didn't answer, I went away.
I thought you were out, that's why!'

The government has announced today
a brand new plan to ensure
that when folk reach the age of sixty
they won't become too poor.

They've introduced a special tax
to be paid by both women and men
to make sure that they all become poor
a long time before then!

The Prime Minister faced a delegation
of squatters at 10 Downing Street.
Two of them opened the door to him
but they wouldn't agree to meet!

LOVELINES!

She told a friend 'My husband
is absolutely dim!
If he was to have a brain transplant
I'm sure it would reject him!'

He said 'I don't know why my wife
buys perfume that's so dear!
It's just a waste of money, because
nobody goes very near!'

'Now that my wife has left me
I just can't sleep' said Noel.
  'She certainly made sure of that
by taking the bed as well!'

  'Why don't our neighbours next door make up?'
  'They should do, I've no doubt,
but unfortunately they can't remember
what they quarrelled about!'

She told her neighbour proudly
  'My husband's doing well.
He's found a job with openings.
He's a doorman in a hotel!'

  'Our teenage daughter caused trouble last night.
She wanted to leave home once more,
but luckily,' he was telling a friend,
  'she only got to the front door.'

  'Then somebody rang, and our daughter spent
over an hour on the phone,
then had her supper, and quite forgot
she'd decided to live on her own!'

CHILDREN SAY THE FUNNIEST THINGS!

Young Sarah was on a ferry one day.
The headmaster said to her
  'If a girl falls overboard, what do you do?'
  'I shout 'Girl overboard sir.'

'That's very good Sarah. Now what would you

do if a school teacher did the same?'
Sarah thought for a moment, then she replied
  'I'd find out the teacher's name!'

'What have you learned at school today?'
she asked her son one night.
James said 'We counted apples up,
and I got them all right.'

He said 'If I had five applies
and then you gave me two,
I'd have seven apples altogether.'
She said 'I'm proud of you!'

  'If I had five bananas, James,
and then you gave me three,
I'm sure that you can tell me
how many there would be?'

At that, James went completely blank
then looked a bit upset.
  'You see' he said at last 'we haven't
done bananas yet!'

Young Tommy wrote to God 'I' sorry
I haven't written before now.
I'm sure that You will understand.
I've only just learned how!'

MEDICAL MATTERS#

The doctor's toilet was blocked up,
so he called the plumber, who said
  'It's Sunday, and it's my day off!
I'll come tomorrow instead.'

The doctor said 'Now my good chap,
that really will not do.
In my job I would come straight okut
on Sunday just for you.'

The plumber finally agreed,
and went to the doctor's that day.
He wasn't there two minutes, but
dealt with it straight away.'

He put three tablets down the toilet,
and then he pulled the chain
then told the doctor 'If it doesn't
clear up, call me again!'

He found his wife was a terrible cook.
He had frozen food every night.
When he went to the doctor as he felt unwell
the doctor said 'You've got frostbite!'

He told the doctor 'I'm getting wed,
and I would like to suggest
that I take this opportunity
to get something off my chest.'

  'You see, I'm marrying Alice.'
The doctor said 'I'm pleased for you.
What do you want to get off your chest?'
  'A tattoo saying I love Sue!'

CHURCH CHUCKLES!

The vicar checked his diary out.
It said '9.30. H C.'
He thought 'It's Holy Communion.
They're waiting at Church for me!'

He dressed appropriately, and went
down to the church straight away.
No one was there! He went back home
saying 'It's a funny day!'

His wife looked quite surprised, and asked
  'Why have you come back here?
You put down in your diary that
you were having your hair cut dear!'

A Bishop gave his bachelor curates
some practical marriage advice.
  'Choose one who is pretty and prudent.
If she has private means that is nice.'

  'Be mindful of your calling, my brothers,
and whatever else you may do,
I'd make sure of the opposite order
of importance, if I was you!'

The first man said 'Our vicar has
got foot and mouth disease!'
His friend replied 'I didn't know
folk had complaints like these!'

The first man said 'Well, he's got it.
He cannot preach at all,
and if you've got a problem, don't
expect him ever to call!'

LIFE'S LIKE THAT

While working in his garden
Fred said to his neighbour Joe
  'Have you forgotten that ten pounds
I lent you a month ago?'

His neighbour gave him a guilty smile,
and said 'No, I haven't yet,
but if you can give me a little more time
I'm sure that I can forget!'

A soldier who lost his rifle
heard his officer say
  'It cost a pretty penny,
and you will have to pay!'

The soldier blinked, then asked him
  'Suppose I lost a tank?'
The officer said 'We'd take away
all that you have in the bank!'

  'If it took the rest of your life
we'd get it back from you!'
The soldier said 'When a ship goes down
I see why the captain drowns too!'

Dave said to his wife 'I wonder why
we never manage to save?'
His wife Maude said 'I blame it on
the neighbours that we have, Dave.'

He looked a little puzzled, until
he heard his dear wife Maud
say 'Well, they're always doing things
that we really can't afford!'

CHILDREN SAY THE FUNNIEST THINGS

'I've got a splinter in my finger'
young Jimmy's sister said.
Jimmy asked, without much sympathy
'Have you been scratching your head?'

'What are sheep who live together?'
young Jimmy asked me today.
I shook my head. 'Pen pals' he chuckled,
before he walked away!

The teacher gave out a maths problem
involving a leaking tap.
She had a very strange answer
from one bright little chap.

She asked 'What is this number,
for I can't make sense of this?'
The lad replied 'It's the phone number
of my dad's plumber, miss!'

A little girl asked her mother one day
'How did I start? Tell me please.'
Her mother had been putting off
answering questions like these.

Quite nervously she said 'You began
life as an egg or a seed.
That's really all there is to it.
Is that the answer you need/'

'That really isn't quite enough'
the shaken mother heard.
'I'm now not sure if I'm a flower,
or if I am a bird!'

CHURCH CHUCKLES!

A Bishop was once on a platform
with a group at a School Speech Day.
The lady presenting the prizes
stood up, then tripped on her way!

The Bishop rushed forward to help her,
and lifted her up from the floor.
 'I have not had a fallen lady'
he said 'in my arms before!'"

She quickly regained her composure
and said 'Bishop, I'm sure that is true.
I've not been picked up by a Bishop,
so this is a first for me too!'

The vicar was a hard working soul.
They offered him a rise.
 'I'd waive it to have Sundays off'
he said to their surprise!

The vicar smiled all down the road,
and a parishioner heard him say
 'I've just made seven people
so really joyful today!'

 'You see, I've done three weddings.
Six dear folk are now wed.'
 'But you said SEVEN joyful souls?'
the puzzled parishioner said.

 'Yes, my dear man' the vicar replied.
 'That certain is true.
You don't think that I married them
without my fees, did you?!'

COFFEE BREAK

'You are a football hooligan,
and I shall sentence you!'
  'On what grounds, your Honour?'
  'Every one that you've been to!'

The policeman stopped an elderly driver
whose progress was erratic and slow.
He said to him 'My dear old chap,
you should wear glasses, you know.;

  'But I've got contacts' the man replied.
At that, the policeman shook his head.
  'I'm not interested in who you know.
Buy a pair of glasses,' he said.

  'Do you know your alphabet?'
  'Yes Miss,' young Jimmy replied.
  'What letter comes after 'A' then?'
  'The rest of them,' Jimmy cried!

He went to pay the restaurant bill
after a very expensive date.
She said 'You don't look very well.
Was it something that I ate?!'

When Mike was at university
the notice was quite clear.
  'Shoes are always required
to eat in the restaurant here.'

He was looking at this notice
when an idea occurred to Mike.
He scribbled below 'But socks may eat
anywhere they like!'

CHILDREN SAY THE FUNNIEST THINGS

His mother caught Jimmy eating,
when he should have been in bed.
'What are you up to?' she asked him.
'My seventh jam tart' Jimmy said!

'Have you seen a man eating tiger?'
young Jimmy was asked one day.
'No, but there's a man eating chicken
in the cafe across the way!'

'Do you know how old your Grandad is?'
somebody asked young Tim.
Tim answered 'No I don't, but Mum
says it's years since we had him!'

Jimmy and Sue were arguing.
'You're stupid!' young Jimmy cried.
'Now say you're sorry' his mother said.
'I'm sorry you're stupid' Jimmy replied.

'I'll teach you to eat your sister's sweets!'
Jimmy's father told his son.
Jimmy replied 'I know how, Dad.
'I've eaten every one!'

Young Jimmy said 'Our holidays
last year were such a bore!
One day the tide went out, and chose
not to come back anymore!'

One question in her exam that day,
a mother was told by her daughter,
was 'What is a liquid that won't freeze?'
and she'd written down 'Boiling water!'

ANIMAL ANTICS

A little girl once went to a zoo,
and threw some pieces of bun.
A stork was nearby, and quite eagerly
gobbled up every one!

The stork then stared at the little girl,
hoping for more buns or bread.
 'What is that bird, Mummy? she asked.
'A stork, dear,' her mother said.

The young girl's face at once lit up,
and she cried excitedly
 'It keeps on looking at me, Mummy.
I'm sure it has recognised me!'

Her husband was reading a magazine.
 'It says in an article here
that over five thousand camels are used
to make paint brushes each year!'

 'I can hardly believe it!' his wife replied,
 'but I suppose it must be true.
Isn't it just amazing, the things
they can teach animals to do?'

Young Jimmy put his tongue out at
the snake he saw in the zoo.
His teacher said 'Now, Jimmy,
that's not the thing to do!'

Jimmy didn't think that was fair,
and said complainingly
 'The snake did it first! It put its tongue
out as soon as it saw me!'

MOTORING MADNESS!

An old lady was driving so badly
her car just twisted and turned.
The driver behind kept his distance
feeling more than a little concerned.

She few to a halt at some roadworks.
He gout out and went to her car
and said 'I am frankly amazed that
you've managed to drive it this far!'

He noticed a dog on the front seat
and continued 'Your driving won't do.
I think if the dog was to drive
it would do much better than you!'

The old lady did not bat an eyelid,
and defiant and quite unimpressed
she replied 'Young man, that's impossible.
The dog hasn't taken the test!'

The driver slowed and called 'Hello.'
A man asked 'Where do you want to go?'
   'Leatherhead' the driver cried.
   'Pigface!' the insulted man replied!

He went to see a foot specialist
as he was in such great pain.
The man examined him and said
   'I'll have you walking again.'

I saw him later, and I said
   'My, you are walking far!'
He answered 'When his bill came in
I had to sell the car!'

LOVELINES!

Grace said 'I think my husband has got
a sympathetic face.
You see, when people look at him
they feel sympathetic' said Grace!

'I got a mink stole for my birthday.'
She said 'My husband really splashed out.
I'm not very sure if it's mink,
but he stole it, of that I've no doubt.'

A budding young actor told his father
'I've got some good news today.
I've just auditioned, and I've been given
my first part in a play!'

'I play the part of a man, Dad,
who's been married for thirty years.'
His father said 'Well done, old chap.
We all have to launch our careers.'

'I hope you will keep on acting.
At least you have made a start.
Perhaps net time you'll be able
to get a speaking part!'

'My mother-in-law uses lemon juice
for her complexion each day.
I think that's the reason' he added
  'why she's so sour in every way!'

'When we go abroad' he said 'my wife
has so many things to say,
she puts suntan lotion on her tongue
before she goes out each day!'

CHURCH CHUCKLES!

'Now vicar, I have a pet parrot'
one dear old parishioner said.
'Round one of his legs is a blue ribbon,
and the other has a ribbon of red.'

'The ribbons help me with my faith, vicar,'
the lady went on to say.
'When my faith is strong I pull the blue ribbon.
It sings Onward Christian Soldiers all day!'

'When I'm feeling weak I pull the red ribbon
and it takes away all my fear,
for the parrot keeps singing the 23rd Psalm
and I know that my Lord is near!'

The vicar said 'My dear that's wonderful,
but what if you pull on the two?'
The parrot called out 'I fall off my perch!
You silly old fool, wouldn't you?!''

The vicar went off to the seaside
on a day when the sun shone bright.
Sadly, he ran out of petrol
before they could get home that night.

He knew of a garage not far away,
so he said to his young family
 'I've got nothing to put any petrol in,
so I'll take baby's potty with me!'

He filled it up, and was pouring it in
when the story goes, so I am told
a motorist slowed, and called 'Vicar, your faith
is an absolute joy to behold!'

LIFE'S LIKE THAT!

A man was pushing a trolley
with a very young child in.
The baby was screaming and crying,
and making an awful din!

The man was endlessly saying
  'Don't get excited, Fred,'
and 'Don't scream, Fred,' and 'Don't yell, Fred,'
and 'Try to keep calm, instead.'

A lady standing next to him
said 'How very kind you are.
You're doing your best to soothe little Fred
before his tantrums go too far!'

The man looked a little bewildered,
then said, 'You've made a mistake.
My name is Fred, and I'm saying all this
only for my own sake!'

I saw a sign in a restaurant
just across the way.
  'Mary had a little lamb.
What will you have today?'

  'Fancy you diving from that height
with all your clothes still on!
To tell the honest truth,' he said
  'I thought my friend was gone!'

He patted the hero on the head.
The hero gave a weak grin,
and then said 'What I want to know
is 'Whoever pushed me in?'

CHILDREN SAY THE FUNNIEST THINGS!

'Count the rings around a tree,'
the teacher said one day,
'and counting one ring for each year
will give its age away.'

When Sue was having tea that day
her mum was firstly told
I'm just not eating that swiss roll,
because it's five years old!'

The teacher told Jimmy 'Your work's a disgrace!
It's just full of mistakes!' he sighed.
'How can you make so many each day?'
'I come early' young Jimmy replied!

He'd just begun an infant school
and came back rather glum.
'There's not much point in going'
the young boy told his mum.

'I can't read yet, and I can't write,
and all through my first week
the lady's told me to be quiet
each time I've tried to speak!'

'What is the outside of a tree?'
the teacher asked young Tim.
Tim shook his head. 'It's bark, boy, bark.'
'Woof-woof' Tim answered him!

'You have an umpire in cricket.
Football has a referee.
Now who do you have in bowls?'
'Goldfish' said Timothy!

FROM THE PARISH MAGAZINE!

Today our Church Secretary
is discussing a new scheme.
It's for anybody suffering
from very low self-esteem.

So my dear friend, if self-esteem
is something that you lack,
please come tonight at half past seven,
but use the door at the back!

Our choir is short of members
and a New Year is beginning,
so please come along and join us
if you are fond of sinning!

There will b e a meeting of little Mothers
on Wednesday at half past three.
Those wishing to become little Mothers
please see the vicar privately!

At the evening service, the vicar
will preach on 'What is Hell?'
If you come along very early
you can hear the choir as well!

On Thursday evening for everyone
we are having a special treat.
We are having a time of fellowship
together as we eat.

Please cook something you can bring
to share with everyone.
A prayer and healing service will follow
after the meal is done!

LIFE'S LIKE THAT!

A nurse was showing a new patient
to his room, and said 'My dear,
now we want you to be happy
and enjoy yourself while you're here.'

'If there is anything you want
you only have to shout,
and if we haven't got it, we'll show
you how to do without!'

He said 'For over twenty five years
I've been selling these wonderful pills.
They are guaranteed to clear up
all of your troubles and ills.'

'I've never had a single complaint,
and each year I've had record sales!
What does that tell you?' A voice in the crowd
called 'Dead men tell no tales!'

'How many words a minute
can you type?' the boss asked Sadie.
'It depends sir, if they're big ones
or little ones' said the lady!

A woman was taking a holiday,
and checking through her list
of people to send postcards to
she told her psychiatrist.

'I'm having a really wonderful time,
and feeling so well and strong.
I only wish that you were here
to tell me what is wrong!'

CHILDREN SAY THE FUNNIEST THINGS!

'I'll give you one hundred apples, Jimmy.
You must give Lucy seven.
Then after Jimmy has had eight
you can then eat eleven.'

'I hope that you've listened carefully,
and that you can answer the question.
Now Jimmy, what are you left with?'
He answered 'Acute indigestion!'

'How do you make a handstand?'
young Jimmy asked me today.
Before I could answer, he told me
　'You take all their chairs away!'

'Who can think of the longest sentence?
Shall we start off with Chris?'
Chris scratched his head, then said 'I know.
Life imprisonment, Miss!'

'What do you run a hundred metres in?'
the games teacher asked young Tim.
　'A tee shirt, shorts and running shoes, Sir,'
the young lad answered him!

'What are you doing near my chocolate cake?'
Summing up the situation,
young Jimmy replied by saying 'Mum,
I'm fighting off temptation!'

The English teacher was doing her best
to teach her class grammar one day.
　'It was getting to be milking time.
What mood?' 'The cow' replied Faye!

MEDICAL MATTERS!

Two girls said 'We've been at university
taking medicine for three years.'
A dear old lady said 'I do hope
that you're better now, my dears!'

A men went off to the doctor's.
 'I've swallowed a light bulb', he said.
The doctor said 'Well, that's a pity,
You must use a candle instead!'

She said 'Doctor, remember I saw you
when my rheumatism was bad.
You told me I must avoid dampness,
and turn up the heating I had.'

 'Well Doctor, I've done all you told me
for the last year and a half.
Now my rheumatism is better
is it all right if I have a bath?!'

 'Will this ointment clear up my spots?'
the anxious lady cried.
 'I never make rash promises
my dear,' the doctor replied!

A shivering patient said 'Doctor,
I think I've gone down with the flu.'
The doctor replied 'Put your tongue out.
See that window? Just put your head through!'

The patient looked rather bewildered.
 'Will that make me better once more?'
The doctor said 'Well, no not really,
'But I can't stand the woman next door!'

LOVELINES!

'Would you like to see where I had my
                    operation?'
Her excited young man cried 'Wow,
I certainly would!' The young lady replied
  'We're passing the hospital now!'

He saw a lady in the street.
She stopped and said 'Hello,'
and then she added 'You're just like
my fifth husband, you know.'

He answered 'Am I really?' and
she told him 'More and more!'
  'How many husbands have you had?'
She said 'Till now, just four!'

'Do you think after thirty five, women
should have children?' she asked her friend.
Her friend said 'After thirty five children
I'd definitely call it the end!'

Two men were chatting in a bar
The first said 'Life's all right!
I used to go to the laundrette,
and get junk food each night.'

  'I wore my socks with holes in them,
and cleaned and made the bed,
until I found a lovely girl
and now I'm happily wed.'

The other man said 'That's funny!
I did the same of course,
but I was so fed up with it
I asked for a divorce!'

ANIMAL ANTICS!

A man walked into a police station and said
  'I'm wondering if you can help me.
I have to live in the same bedroom
as my three older brothers, you see.'

My eldest brother has got seven cats,
and another has got two sheep!
My other brother has got three dogs,
and with the smell, I just can't sleep!'

  'Are there any windows in your room?'
  'Yes, of course there are,' he replied.
  'Well, have you tried opening them, old chap?'
  'What, and lose all my pigeons!' he cried.

Two horses walked into a theatre.
The manager's face was a sight!
One went to the bus office clerk, and said
  'We'd like two stalls for Tuesday night!'

  'Thank you for the goldfish, mum.
I'm really pleased!' said Nell.
  'Tomorrow, I'm looking forward to
getting the bowl, as well!'

  'Dogs must be carried on the escalator'
the department store notice read.
He spent the next two hours looking for one
then gave up, and walked upstairs instead!

Two baby dinosaurs were playing,
when they heard footsteps outside.
One said 'We're supposed to be extinct!
I think we'd better hide!'

CHURCH CHUCKLES!

He drew up a list of church members,
and sent a letter to each.
  'Our vicar is now out of hospital,
but he's still unable to preach!'

A young man preached a sermon,
the very first he'd done.
Next week, the steward asked him
if he'd preach another one.

  'I've only got the one.' The steward
said 'That's fine. You know
nobody will remember what
you said a week ago!'

One lady told the vicar
  'I don't pray every night.
Sometimes I don't need anything
when things are going right!'

A church sign said 'This is God's House.
This is the Gate of Heaven.
We're open Tuesdays 2 till 4
and Sundays 10 till 7!'

  'Each person who comes to our Church Social
will be given a drink and a scone.
Please come along on Saturday night
if you have nothing on!'

A lady said 'I've lost a pound
and it's inside my small son!'
  'Send him to the vicar' they said.
  'He gets money from everyone!'

COFFEE BREAK

I have a rather boastful neighbour,
and only yesterday he said
 'I had a part in a play once.
The play was called 'Breakfast in Bed'.

I wasn't too interested, but asked him
 'Did you have a very big role?'
He replied 'No, just toast and marmalade,'
which I thought quite amusing and droll!

He phoned the landlord who said
 'How can I help you today?'
He said 'It's about the toilet.
I'd like one if I may!'

Our neighbours went to the theatre last night
to see the latest play,
but sadly, they only saw the 1st Act,
and were unable to stay.

 'We bought a programme' said Dolly
 'and when we both looked inside
it said '2nd Act - 2 days later.'
We'd been taken for a ride!'

 'We had to get up and come home.
It seemed rather a crime,
but we couldn't keep our baby-sitter
waiting all that time!'

 'My Grandma plugged her electric blanket
into the toaster' he said,
 'And then she spent the rest of the night
popping out of bed!'

CHILDREN SAY THE FUNNIEST THINGS!

'I've tried to think of a word for two weeks'
the crossword fanatic sighed.
'I know that one. It's a fortnight'
clever young Jimmy replied!

Jimmy said 'My friend's the school swot.'
I asked 'Is he top in each test?'
'No, but he kills a lot of flies,'
said young Jimmy, quite impressed!

Jimmy was driving his mother mad
and putting her on edge.
She told him 'Now it's snowing
let your sister share the sledge!'

Young Jimmy grumbled for a bit,
and then he said 'I will.
I'll go down, and then she can
have it going uphill!'

'Your father can't read the paper,
so go outside and play.'
Young Jimmy said 'I'm only eight,
and I can read OK!'

'There were two chocolate cakes in the larder
when I checked yesterday.
Now there's just one,' Jimmy's mother said,
'so can you explain straight away/'

Jimmy replied 'It was very dark, mum,
when I went downstairs last night.
I must have missed the other one
by not switching on the light!'

SPORTING STORIES!

A group of boys arranged to have
a football match one day.
The match began, then Tim arrived.
They asked 'Why the delay?'

Tim said 'It's Sunday afternoon
you see, and as a rule
my Mum and Dad insist that I
attend our Sunday School.'

'I wanted really badly though
to play this game with you,
and so I thought I'd toss a coin
to see what I should do.'

They said 'We understand all that,
but why were you so long?'
'I tossed it loads of times, because
I kept on calling wrong!'

He thought he would take to the golf course
now that he was newly retired,
and called on the golf professional
to purchase all that he required.

He bought clubs, and a bag and some golf shoes,
an umbrella for rain or for sun,
but when he was asked about golf balls
he answered 'I'll just have the one!'

He returned some weeks later, and heard
'You'll b e wanting some more balls, I bet?'
'Oh no' said the man, 'I don't need them.
I've not hit the first one as yet!'

CHURCH CHUCKLES!

At the vicarage, young Samuel
was the youngest child of four.
His mother said 'Now you are seven
I must go to work once more.'

He found it strange to see her leave
with his father still in bed.
 'What will I do if Daddy gets
a job as well?' he said!

They telephoned the Cricket Club
to ask if the vicar was there.
They said 'He's just gone in to bat,
but no need to despair.'

 'He'll be with you in just a minute.
Of that we are quite sure.
We're really confident, because
we've seen him bat before!'

The vicar was listening to the news
when they spoke of a blizzard that night.
They advised anyone going out
to be clearly seen, and wear white.

The vicar put on his white surplice
and thought 'I'll be really safe now.'
Sadly I have to tell you he was
knocked down by a passing snow plough!

I have nothing but praise for the new vicar'
one old parishioner cried.
 'I noticed that when the offering came round'
the church secretary replied!

LIFE'S LIKE THAT!

His Aunt said 'Jimmy, I'm sorry
you don't like what I've done.
For your birthday, I asked if you would like
a large cheque or a small one.'

Young Jimmy said 'Well, Aunty,
it certainly was a surprise.
I just didn't know that you
were talking about ties!'

A lady said 'These two houseflies
are leading me a merry dance!
I don't know why Noah didn't swat them
when he first had the chance!'

'Waiter, this soup isn't fit to eat!'
The waiter said 'Who told you so?'
  'It was a little swallow
if you really want to know!'

The first pelican said 'I like the fish
that you've got for your tea.'
  'It fits the bill,' the second pelican
replied contentedly!

The driving instructor sighed, and said
  'My friend, I really feel
that you are far too nervous as
you're clutching the steering wheel!'

  'As we still have a few minutes left
of our driving lesson today,
I'll show you how to fill in
the accident forms if I may!'

CHILDRENS PRAYERS

'Did you make up hugging, God?'
little Rachel prayed.
'I think that it's the nicest thing
You have ever made!'

'Dear God, why don't you leave
the sun out at nightfall?
You see, that is the time
I need it most of all!'

'What do you think of plastic flowers?
I think they're really bad,
and if I made real ones like you
I would be very sad!'

'Dear God, I want to tell You that
I like snow better than rain.
I got a sledge for Christmas, so
can You make it snow again?'

'I know You're very busy, God'
young Tim said in his prayer.
'You have to look around and keep
on listening everywhere.'

'My Dad's a vicar, and he talks
about You constantly.
I get enough religion, so
don't worry about me!'

'How often do you pray, my dear?'
Young Sue said 'Once, at night,
because I've never frightened till
Dad switches of the light!'

LOVELINES!

His wife said 'Most accidents happen
in the kitchen, so they say.'
Her husband replied 'I agree, dear.
I'm expected to eat them each day!'

She'd left her husband for the dustman
and told her closest friend,
but said to say, the dustman wouldn't
take him in the end!

'You have the face of a saint' he said.
His wife felt like a Queen,
until he added unkindly
'A Saint Bernard, I mean!'

'Only last week you said that I
was a model husband to you.'
His wife replied 'That description,
I still find perfectly true.'

'For what I have come to realise
is that models are very small,
and in fact they hardly begin to compare
with the real thing at all!'

'We live in a two storey house' he said,
'but things still work out just fine.
She always sticks to her story,
and I always stick to mine!'

He once went out with a girl named Ruth,
but sadly she turned him down flat!
I am sorry to have to tell you
he became ruthless after that!'

CHILDREN SAY THE FUNNIEST THINGS!

Their Grandma was reading her bible.
Young Sue asked her big sister why.
 'She is studying for her final exams'
She heard her big sister reply!

She told the story of our Lord
born on a stable floor.
Young Jimmy said 'It's Joseph's fault.
He should have booked before!'

'Do you know about the Dead Sea?'
the teacher said to Bill.
The boy replied 'I didn't even
know that it was ill!'

A school teacher once asked her class
what they would like to be.
 'A waiter miss' replied young Kate.
The teacher said 'Tell me,
why are you sure that's what you want?'
 'Well teacher,' said young Kate,
my father says that everything
will come to those who wait!'

A little girl once told her mum
 'I've got a pain inside my tum!'
 'It's empty dear' her mum replied
 'because it's got nothing inside.'

The vicar called next day and said
 'I've got a pain inside my head!'
The little girl said 'Not you too!
My mum will tell you what to do!'

COFFEE BREAK

One day young Fred was quite happy
to be given a part in a play,
then they told him 'It is' are the only
two words that you have to say!'

He took his part seriously,
and practised his words day and night.
He'd say then dramatically, thinking
 'At least I shall get my part right!'

Then came the play's opening night.
Fred stood up to say his two words,
then said 'Is it?' instead of 'It is!'
The director thought it quite absurd.

He said 'You have ruined the whole thing!
I only gave you two words, Fred!'
Fred replied 'I don't see a problem.
I knew my part backwards!' he said.

'My wife's been in Boots for twenty five years,'
her husband proudly said.
His friend asked 'Doesn't she take them off
when she gets into bed?'

A young man applied for a credit card.
The manager said 'I'll be frank.
We need to know if you have any
money in the bank.

 'I certainly have!' the young man
replied with a confident smile.
 'Do you know how much?' 'I haven't shaken
the pig for a little while!'

ANIMAL ANTICS!

Some cats were having a milk drinking contest.
The prize went to one of the chaps,
who announced very proudly to all his friends
   'Do you know, I won by six laps!'

The owner of a donkey cart
went to Tim the vet, to say
   'I cannot get my donkey to move.
He just stands still each day!'

The vet replied 'I'll soon fix that.
I've got some medicine here.
Give him three tablespoons right now,
and he'll soon move, don't fear!'

The donkey, after taking it,
went galloping up the lane!
The owner was quite worried that
he wouldn't see him again!

   'It's wonderful!' he told the vet
   'Did you see that donkey go?
It must be marvellous medicine.
Now how much do I owe?'

   'The medicine is ten pounds, sir.'
He said 'Here's twenty more. Tim.
I'd better have two bottles myself,
or I'll never catch up with him!'

   'I thought you said he was house-trained!'
the new dog owner cried.
The previous owner said 'He is.
He never goes outside!'

CHURCH CHUCKLES!

A little boy was laughing
in the middle of a prayer!
His mother turned immediately
and gave her son a glare.

'Be quiet' she whispered crossly.
'That's not the thing to do.'
He answered 'I've told God a joke,
and He is laughing too!'

The new vicar said 'I'm not too pleased
with my meagre salary.
but the fringe benefits are out of this world,
the Bishop keeps telling me!'

'Our church is fairly easy going'
I was told by one sidesman.
'We've five Commandments, and we say
'Do the rest the best you can!'

The Evangelicals were praying
'Lord, set this church on fire.'
'I hope we're well insured' said one,
'or the outcome could be dire!'

A large American car was passing
an old Parish church one day.
The elderly verger was cutting the grass,
and he heard the American say

'Any great men born around these parts?
Friends of mine say that is so.'
The elderly verger scratched his head.
'Only babies, as far as I know!'

MOTORING MADNESS!

She told her husband 'My dear, I bumped
into a neighbour today.
Unfortunately it happened just as
I was backing out of our driveway!'

A policeman was patrolling
a lonely road at night,
when he stopped a motorist, saying
  'You haven't got rear lights!'

The driver held his head, and looked
distraught and very sad.
The policeman feeling sorry, said
  'It's really not that bad.'

  'It's not the lights that worry me'
replied the worried man.
  'Somewhere along the road tonight
I've lost my caravan!'

He said 'I bought a car from you.
It's under guarantee.'
The showroom owner checked his books.
  'Yes sir, I quite agree.'

'We like to please our customers.
I'm sure that you will find
we guarantee all breakages
and parts of every kind!'

  'You have my word, that you don't need
to worry anymore.'
He said 'That's good, because I have
broken my garage door!'

CHILDREN SAY THE FUNNIEST THINGS!

The teacher was telling the story
of David and Goliath one day.
'Why didn't God love Goliath?'
young Jimmy was heard to say!

Young Jimmy started to learn the trombone.
'I'm doing quite well' he said.
'I keep up with all of the others, and
sometimes I finish ahead!'

Young Jimmy once said to his father
 'Can you help with my homework tonight?'
His father did not like that idea,
and he answered 'It wouldn't be right!'

'I don't suppose it would be' said Jimmy
with a mischievous look in his eye.
 'I never get it right either,
but you could at least give it a try!'

Young Jimmy went to his Grandma's
after school to have some tea.
 'Would you like another cookie?' she asked.
 'Yes please' he said eagerly.

His Grandma was quite impressed and said
 'You have good manners, my dear.
 'Please' and 'Thank you' are two expressions
I really do like to hear.'

Jimmy thought for a moment, then he said
 'I'll say both of them for you Gran,
if I could have an extra large piece
of your home made cherry flan!'

LIFE'S LIKE THAT!

She said 'My New Year's resolution
is to be less conceited, you see.
It won't be hard for someone as clear
and intelligent as me!'

'How did you find the weather on holiday?'
Her friend, confused, replied
'I just opened the door of the hotel
and there it was, outside!'

'I met my wife at a dance' he said.
'That's nice' his friend replied.
'She was supposed to be looking after
the children at home' he cried.

A voice called 'Have your tickets ready.
We're doing a spot check.'
One young man said 'If they check my spots
they'll get it in the neck!'

'Jimmy, the school have written to me.
Your handwriting's better, they say.
Your teacher is able to read now
what you write down every day!'

'Sadly, that causes a problem.
Your teacher's quite pleased with you, lad,
but she still doesn't know what you're saying
as your spelling's so terribly bad!'

She said 'My husband is so clever!
He's got enough brains for two!'
Her neighbour rather unkindly said
'Just as well that he married you!'

CHURCH CHUCKLES!

Timothy's mother said 'Say your prayers
on your own now you are ten.'
When she had gone, young Timothy prayed
'Dear God, same as last night. Amen!'

Tim would not eat his rice pudding.
His parents said 'We're cross with you!
Go to your room. When you do wrong
you know God is not pleased with you.'

A short while later a great storm blew up.
Mum was anxious for her little son,
but Dad told her 'He mustn't come down
till he understands what he has done.'

The sky was lit up by lightning,
and it damaged the house next door.
Mum was increasingly worried
till she just couldn't take any more.

'I must go and comfort our Timmy'
she said as she hurried upstairs.
She saw that her young son was kneeling
as if he were saying his prayers.

Then she heard he was saying quite calmly
'I'm sorry Lord, can't You see,
but to make such a fuss over something
like rice pudding, seems stupid to me!'

'Do you believe in free speech?' a tramp asked
as he called at the vicarage one day.
When the vicar said 'Yes,' the tramp continued
'Can I please use your phone straight away?!'

MEDICAL MATTERS!

A couple went to see the dentist.
The husband said 'OK'
no anaesthetic! Just be quick
and take the tooth away!'

The dentist looked admiringly.
 Of all my patients here
I've never met one quite as brave
without a trace of fear!'

'Which tooth is it?' The husband told
his wife 'You show him, dear.
I've got some magazines to read,
so I'll just wait out here!'

'I don't think they know what to do with me,'
a hospital patient said.
 'I've found out that there's a suggestions box
stuck at the end of my bed!'

'What would you take for this cold?'
he asked the doctor one day.
 'Make me an offer, and I'll let you know'
the doctor was heard to say!

He had trouble getting up in the mornings
and his doctor gave him pills to take.
He slept like a log, and then in the morning
he felt rested and so wide awake.

He went to the office and looked at his boss
expecting to hear words of praise.
His boss said 'You're early today, but where
have you been for the last three days?!'

CHILDREN SAY THE FUNNIEST THINGS!

A little boy was saying
that in a book he'd read
all humble bees should never fly
but walk around instead.

Their bodies were too heavy
and their wings were much too short,
so flying, for a bumble bee
was quite a dangerous sport!

But then he burst out laughing
so gaily that he shook.
  'It's just as well that bumble bees
have never read a book!'

A boy helped his grandfather in
the garden one afternoon.
They were digging up potatoes,
but the lad tired of it soon.

  'Grandad' he said 'I don't think I
can do any more today,
but whatever made you bury all
those potatoes anyway?!'

  'Henry the Eighth was furious'
I was told by little Tim,
  'because he found out that the Pope
refused to marry him!'

A little girl wrote 'Armistice was signed
when the end of the war was near,
and ever since then we have all had
two minutes of peace each year!'

LOVELINES!

He had a problem for his wife.
  'What would you do' asked Fred
  'if you were in my shoes, my dear?'
  'I'd polish them' she said!

  'I really am class conscious!' she told
a friend who came to stay.
  'My husband doesn't have any class,
and I'm conscious of it each day!'

She said 'I dress to please my husband.
It pleases him, it appears
if I can make each one I buy
last for at least ten years!'

  'I think you must have a sixth sense'
she said to her husband Clive,
  'because' she added sarcastically
  'There's no sign of the other five!'

She said 'My dearest darling,
you know that coat I wore?
I've seen exactly the same one
on that woman next door!'

Her husband said 'Is that a hint
that you want another one?'
She said 'It's either that, or moving,
when all is said and done!'

  'Darling, if you heard the patter
of tiny feet, would it be nice?'
He said 'I'd move to another house.
I can't stand living with mice!'

LIFE'S LIKE THAT!

She hadn't had her car too long
and didn't like driving at night.
The man behind bumped into her
when she stopped at traffic lights.

No damage was done, and off she went
and stopped at some lights once again.
The man once more bumped into her
and she got out to complain!

She looked at him with pleading eyes,
and then said from the heart
  'If it's not asking too much, please,
can you give me five minutes start?!'

She said 'I haven't seen your son
wearing glasses before.'
  'It seemed a waste. His father
doesn't use them anymore!'

A group of Chinese tourists were in
a safari park one day.
Some lions were watching, and one said
  'Oh look, there's a takeaway!'

The new play was a failure, and
the audience could take no more!
After the first act, most of them
made for the exit door!

One critic said 'I've seen many plays,
and this is really the worst!
Watching the crush, he shouted out loud
  'Women and children first!'

CHURCH CHUCKLES!

Above the pulpit there is a sign
our vicar just dare not ignore.
 'If you can't strike oil in five minutes
then don't continue to bore!'

The bishop stayed at a vicarage
when his conference was done.
No one was more delighted than
the vicar's youngest son.

He asked his father if he could
take the bishop his morning tea.
The vicar said 'All right old chap,
but do it properly.'

 'Knock gently twice upon his door.
Don't make the slightest row.
Just say 'It is the boy, My Lord.
It's time to get up now.'

The boy repeated what he'd heard,
and practised it so long
that he was sure when morning came
he couldn't get it wrong.

He knocked upon the bishop's door
clutching the special cup,
then called 'It is the Lord, my boy,
and now your time is up!'

 'Three cheers for the vicar' someone cried,
and a little boy named Hugh
said 'I hope he'll find them more comfortable
than this hard old wooden pew!'

ANIMAL ANTICS!

A woodpecker was pecking a hole in the tree
while a storm raged all around.
A fork of lightning struck the tree
and felled it to the ground.

The woodpecker looked rather shocked,
and then it said at length
  'Well, fancy that! Quite obviously
I don't know my own strength!'

  'Mum, we went to the zoo today!
Our teacher took us there.
There were lions and tigers and monkeys,
and a lovely polar bear.'

  'We saw the elephants as well
I really do like zoos!
In two separate enclosures
we saw a lot of gnus.'

  'Why are they separated?'
Her son said from the heart
  'Because there's good gnus and bad gnus
they have to live apart!'

There was a naughty monkey named May
who argued all day long.
One day she quarrelled with a lion,
and lions are very strong!

I'd like to write a little more,
but I must end quite soon.
You see, that was the end of May.
Tomorrow's the 1st of June!

SOMETHING TO THINK ABOUT

'What's your opinion of my painting?'
he asked a critic one day.
'It's worthless.' The artist said 'I know,
but give me it anyway!'

The engine driver's bride looked lovely
as she waited at the church gate,
but her train unfortunately
was twenty five minutes late!

A compiler of crossword puzzles has died.
His friends mourned his tragic loss,
then after a service they buried him
six down and three across!

Most accidents happen in your home
so if things don't improve,
perhaps the only answer might be
to pack your bags and move!

Committees may be important.
They may have special powers.
Most of them make minutes
but all of them take hours!

I saw a Church notice the other day
I thought was rather appealing.
'Have you a long standing problem?
Can we suggest you try kneeling?'

Let your sermon have a good beginning
and a good ending, whatever you do,
and you'll find it will be even better
when there's less time between the two!

CHILDREN SAY THE FUNNIEST THINGS

The vicar said to one young girl
'You're not a regular here.'
The girl replied 'I'm regular,
at Christmas every year!'

She looked at her naughty Grandson,
and in despair she cried
'What kind of children go to Heaven?'
'The dead ones' he replied.

When Father Christmas went around
a hospital one day
a little girl tugged at his cloak
in a really eager way.

'You're just a little impatient.
Wait till I get to you.'
She said 'No, I'm an 'er patient.
Your eyes need testing too!'

A little girl at school once wrote
'Soon after I was born
I realised that my mum and dad
were getting old and worn.'

'Although I did my very best
and tried for days and days,
I had to give up in the end.
They wouldn't change their ways!'

The vicar said one Christmas Day
'All God's creatures are joyful today.'
One little boy stood up to say
'A turkey won't feel quite that way!'

COFFEE BREAK

Grandpa said 'Today I bumped
into a friend of Grandma's.
He added 'It's just a pity
that we were both in our cars!'

Stella quite wanted a squirrel fur coat,
but her enthusiasm was waning
as a friend had told her it could be ruined
if she wore it when it was raining.

The manager spoke reassuringly,
saying 'Don't worry' to Stella.
   'After all, my dear, have you ever seen
a squirrel with an umbrella?!'

'Our Jimmy might be an astronaut!'
she told her best friend Grace.
   'I spoke to his teacher only today,
and she says he's taking up space!'

'You landed your plane on top of a house!
Had your fuel all gone?'
   'No,' the pilot said, 'but I saw
that the landing lights were on!'

A man with a newt on his shoulder
went into a public bar.
He said 'I call my pet 'Tiny,'
and he sleeps in an old jamjar.'

The barman to humour him, told him
   'Your creature is really quite cute,
but why do you call him 'Tiny?'
The man said 'Because he's my newt!'

CHURCH CHUCKLES!

A vicar was leaving after many years
and a farewell was held in the hall.
The church secretary was giving a speech
and said thank you to one and all.

Then he remembered those folk who were
unable to attend that day.
  'Some are sick and some are sad'
the secretary felt led to say.

'And some have never loved thee well'
muttered one spirited lad,
and quoting the same hymn, he added
  'Some have lost the love they had!'

A vicar in a hospital
had many folk to see.
He moved from ward to ward, then went
into Maternity.

He asked one lady lying there
  'Have you been confirmed, my dear?'
She answered, quite surprise 'Of course!
That's why I am in here!'

An emergency in the parish
occurred when the vicar was ill.
They asked the bishop to preach
and he replied gladly 'I will.'

The churchwardens wrote, saying 'Bishop,
a poorer preacher would have done,
but despite our very best efforts
none of us here could find one!'

CHILDREN SAY THE FUNNIEST THINGS!

A vicar was asking the Bishop to lunch,
and said to his eight year old son
  'Be polite, and if he asks questions,
as you answer, add 'My Lord, to each one.'

The lunch came and went, and the Bishop
did not speak till the meal was through,
then he said to the terrified youngster
  'Hello young man. How old are you?'

The young boy had not met a Bishop,
and had worked himself into a state.
Forgetting the words of his father
he answered him 'My God, I'm eight!'

He asked his teenage son one day
  'Do you think about God, my lad?'
His son said 'yes, but not as much
as my clothes and my new girl friend, dad!'

A teacher spoke to her children
on Harvest Festival Day.
She asked some of the children
to name food on display.

They called out 'carrots, cabbages,
potatoes, beans and peas.'
  'Good,' said the teacher 'can you give
one word that covers these?'

There was a silence, then she said
  'Surely someone knows this.'
Young Jimmy slowly raised his hand.
  'I think it's gravy, miss!'

LIFE'S LIKE THAT!

I met a friend who told me
just yesterday afternoon
 'My sister from Australia
is coming home quite soon!'

His eyes were misting over,
and through his joy and tears
he said 'I haven't seen Doris
for forty seven years!'

He said 'I have this nagging doubt
that worries me somehow.
After all the years, will I
still recognise her now?'

I said to him 'I understand,
and what you say is true,
but she may have a problem
in recognising you!'

This thought had not occurred to him,
because I heard him say
 'Of course she'll know me! For a start
I haven't been away!'

His manners were impeccable
and he cared for folk a lot.
He gave a lady his seat on a bus
but she fainted on the spot!

When she came round, she told the man
 'You really are a saint!'
Not used to being thanked, she found
it was his turn to faint!

CHURCH CHUCKLES!

The plane was at forty thousand feet
when an announcement was made.
  'Two of our engines have just failed.
Our flight will therefore be delayed.'

  'Fasten your safety-belts now please
and put out your cigarettes.
Although we have an emergency
there's no need to panic or fret.'

Yet one of the passengers panicked
and seeing a vicar on board
he called out 'Do something religious!
This crisis cannot be ignored!'

The vicar took heed of this person
and thought he should help him somehow.
  'Very well, my good friend' he responded.
  'We'll take up a collection right now!'

Young Jimmy asked me just today
  'What does God have for tea?'
I shook my head, and he then said
  'Angel cakes,' full of glee!

Susan had never been to church
and saw folk kneeling down.
  'What are they doing, Mummy?'
she asked with a puzzled frown.

  Be quiet my dear' her mother said.
  'They're all saying their prayers.'
  'They've got their clothes on! Can't they wait
until they go upstairs?!'

LOVELINES!

A confident young man approached a girl,
and asked in a voice so polite
  'I just wondered if you were eating
anywhere at all tonight?'

The young girl was rather embarrassed,
and felt her face go a bright red!
  'No, not that I know of' she answered.
  'You'll be hungry tomorrow' he said.

  'Your husband cares for you terribly!'
she said when they met for a chat.
  'I know he does' the wife replied.
  'I'm always telling him that!'

She said 'I've been wed for thirty odd years.'
Her friend asked 'Why odd? Please explain.'
She replied 'If you met my husband
you would not ask that question again!'

She told a neighbour down the road
  'I collect antiques, you know.'
Her neighbour said 'That's right. I met
your husband a week ago!'

  'I'll open a bank account Mrs Jones.
You'll want a joint account, no doubt?'
  'That's right' she said. 'My husband pays in
and I'll be drawing it out!'

  'Do you still work for the same bosses?'
she asked her neighbour Bill.
  'Oh, you mean the wife and children?
Yes, I work for them still.'

CHILDREN SAY THE FUNNIEST THINGS!

She'd never been to church, until
her mum took her one day.
  'Be still and know that I am God'
she heard the vicar say.

She'd listened very carefully
and felt herself go numb.
She whispered very thoughtfully
  'Gosh, is he really, Mum?!'

A large and friendly dog one day
bounced up to little Guy.
He licked Guy's face and hands, and caused
the little lad to cry.

  'Did he bite you?' Guy's mother asked
her son consolingly.
  'No' sobbed the child 'he didn't bite,
but mum, he tasted me!'

The teacher said 'Jimmy, if you mowed lawns
For twenty people you met,
and each of them gave you five pounds
then what, my lad, would you get?'

Jimmy had never been good at maths
but he called out 'Yes, I know this.
If twenty people gave me five pounds
I'd get a new bicycle, miss!'

Jimmy said 'I've added your sums up ten times.'
The teacher replied 'Thanks a lot.'
Jimmy continued 'Now do you want
to know the ten answers I got?!'

COFFEE BREAK

When Joe went off for an interview
The boss said 'Now I'm aware,
that life is giving and taking,
so both of us must be fair.'

'When you have a good employer
you can't do too much, you know.'
'Don't worry, there's not much chance of that'
replied the work-shy Joe!

'I want somebody quick to take notice.'
Young Joe was not short of cheek!
He said 'That shouldn't be hard for me.
I was given it twice last week!'

He said 'I will need a reference.'
Joe replied 'Mine is good, without doubt.
My last employer said I was the best
that he had ever turned out!'

A burglar stopped to have a shower
as he robbed a house one day.
When the police asked him, he said he wanted
to make a clean getaway!

Bill, who was a very big business tycoon
had a secretary who was quite tall.
She took dictation in longhand,
and then he had one who was small.

She took dictation in shorthand,
and he had one tinier still!
She used to write the footnotes
for her high powered boss named Bill!

ANIMAL ANTICS!

A man walked into the jungle
and played on his flute one night.
The monkeys and tigers came along
and listened with pure delight!

The cheetahs sat down with the leopards
and the elephants gathered around.
All of the birds stopped singing,
and enjoyed this lovely sound.

Suddenly a great big lion approached,
and ran through the gathered crowd.
He gobbled up the man, and then sat down,
feeling very smug and proud!

The animals were very cross, saying
  'We were all enjoying hearing him play!'
  'Pardon?' the lion said, cupping his ear,
  'I just can't hear a word you say.'

The first flea said 'You don't look too well.
I won't come very near.'
The second flea said 'You're right. I'm not
feeling up to scratch, my dear!'

I took my dog out this morning.
We saw 'Wet Paint' on a sign.
He did, and I do wish sometimes
that my dear dog wasn't mine!

She cried 'An elephant's robbed the bank!'
  'Would you recognise it?' the policeman said.
  'I'm not really sure I would' she replied.
  'It had a stocking over its head.'

CHURCH CHUCKLES!

The curate said to the parish priest
  'There's a man at the back, can you see?
He's very old with a long white beard,
and He's God, or so he tells me!'

  'Well, I declare!' said the parish priest.
The curate said 'What shall I do?'
  'Keep an eye on him, and I'd also try
to look busy if I was you!'

A visiting preacher was very short!
In fact, from the pulpit they said,
the folk at the back of the church
could just see the top of his head.

He preached with a passion and fervour!
  'I'm the Lamp of the Lord!' he cried.
  'Turn your wick up. We can't see you,'
a lady at the back replied.

A girl from the Salvation Army
saw a saloon bar, and she entered in.
She mingled with all the folk in there,
shaking her collecting tin.

She walked up to a very old man
who asked 'What are you doing here?'
  'I'm collecting for our dear Lord' she said.
  'I call once a week through the year.'

The elderly man then smiled and said
  'It's a wonderful work that you do!
If you'd like to give me the tin, my dear,
I'll be seeing the Lord before you!'

MEDICAL MATTERS!

He told a patient 'There's nothing much wrong.
It must be the drink' he said.
The patient replied 'Doctor, I understand.
I'll come back when you're sober instead!'

The doctor asked one anxious man
  'Now sir, how do you feel?'
  'Doctor, I'm getting indigestion
immediately after each meal!'

'It might seem rather strange to you,
but to start with I have to say
I am quite fond of snooker balls
and enjoy eating them every day!'

'I normally start every meal
with a yellow one then a brown,
then I have a blue and pink and black
to wash all my dinner down!'

'That is the reason' the doctor said,
  'why you are not full of beans.
The problem you see is that you are
not having any greens!'

'Doctor, my little boy's swallowed ten pence!'
The doctor said 'That's rather strange,
but keep him in bed for just a few days
and I'm certain you'll see some change!'

'Take a bath before you retire'
the doctor told young Clive.
  'Gosh Mum, I needn't have one till
I'm nearly sixty five!'

CHILDREN SAY THE FUNNIEST THINGS!

A little boy went off to church.
He'd never been before,
and as he left he saw the vicar
standing at the door.

The young lad said to him 'Vicar,
I think you've got things wrong.
I liked the music, but I thought
the adverts were too long!'

'Funerals are very useful'
said a little boy one day,
' because they help to let God know
that you are on your way!'

A little girl was listening
when the vicar's talk began.
The vicar said 'Now I am proud
to be a self made man.'

The young girl whispered 'Daddy,
he's really much too fat.
I wouldn't be so proud if I
had made myself like that!'

'How will you get to heaven?'
she asked her naughty son.
'I'll keep on running in and out
upsetting everyone!'

'Then I will slam the door until
their patience wears quite thin,
and they'll say 'Come in or stay out!'
and that's when I'll go in.!'

LIFE'S LIKE THAT!

He wanted to decorate his lounge
to give his wife a surprise.
He knew his neighbour had just done his
and their lounges were both the same size.

'How many rolls of wallpaper
did you purchase to do the job?'
'I went and bought eight to do the lounge'
he was told by his neighbour Bob.

He only needed five rolls of wallpaper,
and he wasted the other three!
He told his neighbour who said 'That's right.
The same thing happened to me!'

She gave the bus driver a twenty pound note.
'Is that all you've got?' he sighed.
She smiled at the driver so sweetly.
'I've more in the bank' she replied.

The foreman of the factory was
interviewing a man.
He asked him 'Can you make the tea?'
The man replied 'I can.'

'Now, can you drive a fork lift truck?'
He said 'No, I cannot,'
but then he added in surprise
'How big is your teapot?!'

'I do not recognise this court!'
they heard the defendant cry.
'Now, why is that?' the judge asked him.
'It's been decorated, that's why!'

CHURCH CHUCKLES!

A vicar and a taxi-driver
both died on the very same day.
The taxi-driver went to heaven,
but the vicar was kept away!

The vicar grumbled at St Peter
and said 'It's most unfair.
While he was driving folk around
I spent my day in prayer!'

'That may be so' St Peter said,
'but we work differently!
While you were giving a service
people fell asleep, you see!'

'But when the taxi-driver gave
a service, yes folk paid,
but we have also noticed that
nearly everybody prayed!'

They had a meeting in their church
and said 'We'd like to see
a banner telling everyone
about the Nativity.'

They told the secretary
 'We'll leave it up to you
to tell the banner maker
exactly what to do.'

So she sent him a telegram,
concerned he might get it wrong.
 Unto us a Son is born.
Two feet wide and eight feet long!'

MOTORING MADNESS!

An American tourist came to London
to have a holiday.
He was talking to an Englishman
in such a boastful way.

'Back home' he said 'I'm telling you,
my lifestyle is just great.
It takes me several hours to drive
around my huge estate!'

The Englishman was not impressed
with all his pompous chat!
He said 'I sympathise, for I
once had a car like that!'

'Can you please check my tyres?' he asked
the garage attendant he saw.
The attendant had a quick glance, then said
   'Yes sir, you've still got all four!'

An American went to Ireland
and saw all the lovely sights.
He was impressed with the bleeping sounds
that he heard at traffic lights.

'Say, what is that?' he enquired of his host.
His host replied 'We've designed
a system with the bleeping, that
will benefit those who are blind.'

The American was really touched,
and said, humbled and feeling small,
   'Back home, blind folk are not allowed
to drive a car at all!'

CHILDRENS PRAYERS

One school day Jimmy overslept
and woke at half past eight.
He hurried off to school, and prayed
　'Dear God, don't make me late!'

Then suddenly he tripped and fell
and landed in a bush.
Quite crossly, Jimmy prayed once more
　'God, there's no need to push.'

'Thank You for my baby brother.
I wanted a puppy from You,
but I know You are very busy, God,
so for now a brother will do!'

'If we come back as somebody else'
young Jimmy was heard to pray,
　'don't let me come back as Tommy, God,
for he keeps hitting me each day!'

'God, thank You for the stories you wrote'
Tom prayed. 'I like the rest
but the ones about Noah and David
I really enjoyed the best!'

'If Cain and Abel had had their own rooms
they wouldn't have needed to fight.
It has worked out for me and my brother
for at least a whole fortnight!'

A little girl prayed 'Dear God above,
take care, whatever You do,
because we'll all be in a mess
if anything happens to You!'

LOVELINES!

Her young man was to take her out.
She waited an hour and a half!
Realising that he wouldn't come
she was in no mood to laugh!

She changed into her casual clothes
and put her slippers on.
She made some sandwiches, and thought
  'Today will soon be gone!'

Just then the doorbell rang, and she
saw her young man standing there.
Before she was able to say a word
he cried 'I do despair!'

 'I had a problem on the way,
and I know I'm two hours late,
but look at you! I see you're still
not ready for our date!'

He asked his friend 'Does your good wife
believe in love at first sight?'
He said 'Since she's had a mirror
she's believed in that, all right!'

A young man thought he'd take a chance
and asked quite nervously
  'Now, do you think that you could be
happy with a man like me?'

At first she said quite cheerfully
  'My dear, of course I do,'
and then after thinking, she said 'as long
as he isn't too much like you!'

CHILDREN SAY THE FUNNIEST THINGS!

Aunt Susan from Australia
came for a holiday.
Her little niece had never met
her till she came to stay.

When asked her name, the lady said
  'Aunt Susan, from afar.'
  'If you aren't Susan' said the girl,
  'please tell me who you are!'

A little boy said to his friend
while paddling in the sea,
  'It really doesn't look as if
you've washed for months to me.'

The second boy, quite unabashed
replied at once to him.
  'Well, after all, it's been a year
since I last had a swim!'

The teacher said to Johnny 'Can
you tell me an animal's name?
It gives us food and also clothes,
and it's really soft and tame.'

She waited for the answer 'Lamb'
to come from this young lad,
but Johnny thought for a moment, then
he said 'It must be Dad!'

A bald young man had a black bushy beard.
One little boy stared, with a frown
and then he said 'Dad, can you tell me,
why is his head upside down?!'

COFFEE BREAK

'How long does it take to fly to New York?'
he asked the airport operator.
   'Just a minute' she said. 'Thanks very much!
I thought I would get there much later!'

People were being thrown to the lions!
The Emperor said 'There's no hitch.
This is a sport where we never have
spectators running on to the pitch!'

The diner had waited for ages,
then got a squashed apple pie!
   'You asked me to step on it, sir,'
said the waiter, with a gleam in his eye!

   'I want to be a bus driver'
young Jimmy said one day.
His father quickly answered
   'I won't stand in your way!'

The tug of war team lost their final
match, or so it is said,
because they all forgot the rules
and started to push, instead!

   'There are twenty pubs in our town'
he told his teenage son,
   'and I'm quite happy to tell you
that I've never been in one!'

The youth looked at his father.
   'Well, Dad, we can put that right.
Tell me which one you haven't been in,
and we'll both go there tonight!'

ANIMAL ANTICS!

The young man knew his aged aunt
was a very wealthy soul,
and setting out to please her, soon
became a major goal!

She had two poodles that she loved
and they needed exercise.
He didn't care much for them, but
sought favour in her eyes.

'I'll walk them for you, dearest aunt'
she heard her nephew say,
and sure enough, he came around
and took them out each day.

He thought 'I'm sure that in her will
she will remember me.
I'm certain that I'll be a major
beneficiary!'

One day his aged aunt died, but
the news was pretty grim!
He didn't get a penny piece
but she left the dogs to him!

An advert read 'Alsations for sale.
Phone up and ask for Joe.
They are very fond of people.
Reluctant to let go!'

The patient told the doctor
 'I have got a little stye.'
The doctor said 'My friend has got
a pig you might like to buy!'

CHURCH CHUCKLES!

Fred cycled off to his local pub
to have a drink one night.
He was having supper with his wife
when he realised things weren't right.

'I left my bicycle at the pub
and I walked back home' he said!
 'It was nearly new, and you haven't a lock.
You've lost that!' his wife told Fred.

Fred hurried back and saw his bicycle
leaning against the wall.
He started to ride home thinking
 'That was a really close call!'

He passed a church and it made him think
of a debt to be repaid.
 'I must thank God for his kindness,'
so he went inside and prayed.

He put a donation in the box,
then thought 'I must hurry on,'
but when he got outside he saw
that his bicycle had gone!

 'Granny's rheumatism's not good,
and it's such cold weather that we've had.'
 'Dear Lord, make it hot for Grandma,'
prayed her obedient lad!

 'We had a lovely church gathering
last Tuesday, at half past three.
The ladies committee, with enthusiasm
threw themselves into the tea!'

COMPANIONSHIP!

She said 'I'm very lonely.
I said 'I'm lonely too.
We could be together, if
we've nothing else to do.'

She said 'I'll check my diary.
Just look, there's nothing there.'
I said 'Mine is just the same.
I've got a whole day spare.'

She said 'Well, that's okay then,
We'll have a cup of tea.'
I said 'That's a good idea.
Now you must come to me.'

She said 'It's nice to get out.
I should get out much more.'
I said 'It isn't very far.
I only live next door.'

She said 'I'll come to you then.'
I said 'You'll see my cat.
Then we'll have a cup of tea
and have a lovely chat.'

She stayed until the evening
my cat upon her knee.
She talked to it the whole day,
but never spoke to me.

She said 'Perhaps tomorrow?'
I said 'Another day.'
I'm used to being lonely
in my own special way!

CHILDREN SAY THE FUNNIEST THINGS!

A little girl was drawing
when her Grandma came to call.
The young child asked 'Did you have crayons
Grandma, when you were small?'

Her Grandma smiled, and answered her
  'Yes, I had crayons all right.'
The girl said 'Grandma, I expect
that yours were black and white!'

A little girl was bored one day
with nothing much to do,
and so a kindly aunt took her
around the local zoo.

She found the leopards' cage quite soon,
and leopards she adored,
but then she saw the words 'Wet Paint'
were written on a board.

She showed a disappointment that
her aunt could really feel.
  'I thought' the little girl told her
  'that all their spots were real!'

While driving down a road one day
I told my little son
  'Along this stretch of road I once
collided with someone.'

  'We had to swap our names for our
insurance claims you see.'
  'So what are you called now, daddy?'
my little boy asked me!

LIFE'S LIKE THAT!

He used to keep a tractor
with spare parts everywhere.
His wife put up with this for years
till she was in despair.

She said to him 'You'll have to choose
between that thing and me,
or else I'm leaving you right now!
So what is it to be?'

He loved her very much, and so
he gave the lot away
but then an accident occurred.
A fire broke out next day!

While working in the garden
He heard his scared wife shout.
He took a deep breath, till the flames
and smoke were all sucked out!

She said in awe 'I'm really glad
I married such a man.'
He said 'It's nothing, for you see
I'm an ex-tractor fan!'

She saw her neighbour's little boy
and said 'He is a dear!
How old is he?' The mother said
  'My Billy's just one year.'

'He's really quite advanced. He's walked
for four months now, you know!'
Her neighbour said 'He must be tired!
Wherever did he go?'

CHURCH CHUCKLES!

The vicar was trying to organise
the Christmas Nativity Play,
but was having a great deal of trouble
finding a suitable day.

At last, one old lady advised him
  'We'll never agree, that's quite clear.
Can we have it when we're not so busy,
some other time in the year?!'

They found that the church roof was leaking.
The church warden said 'There's no doubt
we have a large drip in the pulpit,
but hopefully we'll sort things out!'

A lady asked to join his church
and so the Catholic priest
thought 'I had better test her out
about divorce at least.'

He asked her 'If your marriage, dear
should prove to be unsound,
would you consider marrying
a second time around?'

The lady blushed, then answered him
  'I wouldn't, no thank you,
but it was certainly quite nice
of you to ask me to!'

He rang the Salvation Army to ask
  'You have young girls, I see.
I'm wondering if on Saturday
you could save one for me!'

SERVICE WITH A SMILE!

The local vicar was so kind
and friendly and polite.
He took a dear soul in his church
down to the station one night.

He parked beside the taxi rank.
She thanked him for the ride.
Before the vicar could drive off
a lady jumped inside!

'The Grand Hotel' she said to him,
'and get their quickly please.'
The vicar wasn't really used
to situations like these!

He drove about ten miles until
They reached the Grand Hotel.
She got a twenty pound note out
and said 'You drove so well!'

He said 'I'm just a vicar, dear.'
She said 'Oh silly me!
Well, put this in your collection please,'
and gave him 50p!

The vicar thanked her for her gift
and went to drive away.
She tapped upon his window
as she'd something else to say.

He wound the window down, and heard
her say 'You are a dear!
Can you come back at midnight please
and pick me up from here?'!

CHILDREN SAY THE FUNNIEST THINGS!

A bishop visited a manse
in which a vicar stayed.
The vicar went to make the tea
while his young daughter played.

She thought the bishop seemed quite nice,
and shyly took his hand.
 'Please tell me something that my dad
just cannot understand.'

The bishop, feeling pleased and proud
said 'Well my dear, I'll try.
Now, what is it you want to know.
There's no need to be shy.'

 'Well, what my dad just can't work out'
he heard her sweetly say,
 'was how on earth the church made you
a bishop anyway!'

A Sunday School teacher was asking her class
 'Can anyone answer this?
When Goliath met David, what can we learn?'
Said Jimmy 'That we should duck, miss!'

A girl on a bus kept sniffing
and the man next to her sighed.
He asked 'Have you got a hankie?'
 'Yes' the little girl replied.

 'My mother's told me not to speak
to strangers such as you,
so I'm really very sorry
but you cannot borrow it too!'

LOVELINES!

His wife stepped on a weighing machine
which read her fortune too.
Her face lit up with happiness
the moment she read it through.

'It says I'm most attractive
with a warm personality.
It also says that I can charm
each person that I see!'

Her husband took the card from her,
and said 'I hate to tell,
apart from everything you've said
your weight is wrong as well!'

'I'd like to buy the woman I love
a cottage by the sea.'
His friend said 'Well, what's stopping you?'
'My wife just won't let me!'

'We've had two happy, glorious years'
she said to her husband Clive.
'Mind you' she continued
'we've been married for twenty five!'

I asked her father if we could marry
and he said 'Leave your name and address,
and if nothing better comes up, then
you can marry my daughter Tess!'

He said 'I think my wife is hoping
that I'll go away.
She wrapped my sandwiches for lunch
up in a road map today!'

COFFEE BREAK

A little Australian boy was given
a new boomerang for his birthday.
I am told he spent the next fortnight
throwing his old one away!

'My Lord, the prisoner is deaf!'
The judge said 'I'm disappearing.
You know you can't condemn someone
without a proper hearing!'

The burglar tried to flee, but got
stuck in wet cement somehow.
They tell me that the burglar's
a hardened criminal now!

'Don't pour hot water down a rabbit hole!
'It's really not very funny,
and if you do, you're likely to see
at least one hot cross bunny!

'I used to be a fortune teller,
but that was in the past.
There wasn't any future in it'
he said, 'I decided at last!'

Two fishermen were in their boat
when a hand appeared in the sea!
'Is someone drowning?' 'No, it looked
like a little wave to me!'

'Now wipe that mud off your shoes
before you come indoors, Penny!'
She looked at her mother and said
'But Mum, I'm not wearing any!'

MEDICAL MATTERS!

Now Mr Brown was eighty six
and feeling rather poorly.
He told the doctor that deep breaths
affected him quite sorely.

The doctor checked him thoroughly
and said 'Your heart's quite dicky,
but then you see at your great age
things start to get quite tricky.'

'There's nothing I can do for you
but maybe you should try Brown
to drink a double whisky first
before you go and lie down.'

He saw the doctor in a week
and said 'I'm really happy.
Why, since I've taken your advice
I've felt a different chappie.'

'I've had the double whisky, then
laid down as you suggested.
About eight times a day, I've had
a drink then gone and rested!'

A men went to the doctor
and said 'I cannot sleep.'
The doctor asked his patient
  'Have you tried counting sheep/'

He answered 'That's the trouble.
I count, and each mistake
just means I have to count again
and spend the night awake!'

ANIMAL ANTICS!

The animal trainer had a new act,
with a dog that sang all day,
and a cat that played the piano
in a very expert way!

The audience came from miles around
and the trainers fame soon grew,
for people love to see something
that's clever and quite new.

The act was seen one evening by
an impresario.
By watching carefully, he said
 'I've worked it out, you know.'

He told the trainer how he'd noticed
every single bit.
The trainer nodded rather sadly
and then admitted it.

The trainer said 'I thought at last
someone like you would guess.
The cat does everything because
he's a ventriloquist, I confess!'

An advert read 'Alsations for sale.
Phone up and ask for Joe.
They are very fond of people.
Reluctant to let go!'

She had a dog that always growled, and
a cat that came home late each night.
What with a parrot that talked all day long
she said 'Marriage just wouldn't be right!'

CHURCH CHUCKLES!

The vicar approached a parishioner
and gave him a friendly smile.
 'We haven't seen you at the church'
he said 'for quite a while.'

He replied 'My youngest daughter
is learning the harp, you see.
I've had second thoughts about Heaven'
 he added ruefully!

A decorator charged for paint,
then cheated everyone.
He watered down the paint, and so
each job was cheaply done.

He got away with it until
a voice filled him with awe.
The voice called out to him 'Young man,
repaint and thin no more!'

I saw a notice in our church
that read 'When Summer begins
we'll tackle one at a time on Tuesdays
the seven deadly sins!'

A vicar was due to leave his church
and went round to say goodbye.
One dear old lady was quite upset,
and spoke with a tear in her eye..

 'Vicar, we're sorry to see you go.
I don't like to make a fuss,
but all the old women will miss you so.
We feel you are one of us!'

SOMETHING TO THINK ABOUT

A man who taught philosophy
once thought he'd cross the street,
and he started very boldly,
striding out with both his feet.

He reached the middle, then he stopped,
unable to decide
which foot he should continue with..
A car came, and he died!

The moral of this story should
be clear to everyone.
Making the wrong decision may
be better than making none!

Henry the Eighth married six times.
Some people thought it strange
until the King explained to them
he liked to chop and change!

A friend of mine who's just retired
was never short of cheek.
He's never had a day's illness.
He'd make it last a week!

A second hand shop had a sign
that really caught my eye.
  'We sell the best antiques around,
though it's rubbish that we buy!'

Remember, every visitor
brings pleasure to the heart.
It's either when they enter in
or else when they depart!

CHILDREN SAY THE FUNNIEST THINGS!

'We fight with words and not with deeds'
Tom's parents used to say.
He told his mother after school
'Mum, Jack hit me today!'

His mother sympathised, then said
'Violence cannot succeed!
I hope you told him that we fight
with words and not with deeds!'

Tom thought a while, and then replied
'I said all that to Jack,
but he just took no notice, so
I went and hit him back!'

A mother drove her little girl
to stay with some friends for tea.
Her daughter said 'When we drive home
can you sit in the back with me?!'

Young Christopher was promised
a day trip to the zoo.
His father had a day off work
and he was going too.

The day came round, and Christopher
Just hadn't learned to wait!
He worried that his Daddy
might get up far too late.

He crept into his bedroom,
and anxious and upset
he lifted his Daddy's eyelids
and asked 'Are you in yet?!'

LIFE'S LIKE THAT!

A tenant had a leaking roof
which she asked her landlord to repair.
I asked her if he'd done it yet.
  'No' she replied in despair.

  'What's more' she said despondently,
  'he gets meaner by the hour!
He wants to charge me extra rent
now that I've got a shower!'

A neighbour said to Jimmy's mum
  'I'm very cross! You see
your son is coming to my gate
and imitating me!'

She sympathetically replied
  'Yes, that is rather cruel,'
then added quite ambiguously
  'He mustn't act the fool!'

She saw her young son with a three piece suite,
and said 'You're aware of the dangers!
How many times have I told you, my lad,
you must never accept suites from strangers?!'

  'Tomorrow you will fly solo'
the flying instructor told him.
  'How low?' the trainee pilot asked,
looking quite tense and grim!

A customer went to a record shop.
  'Have you got 'Greensleeves' my dear?'
  'No Madam' the salesperson answered.
  'It's just the strip lighting in here!'

CHURCH CHUCKLES!

A vicar was due to leave his church.
At a lunch to say goodbye
one dear old soul was overcome
and she began to cry.

'Don't fret my dear' the vicar said.
'Trust God and you will see
He'll send another vicar soon
you'll like as much as me.'

Indignantly she wiped her eyes.
'I'd like to think that's true,
but when the one before you left
he said the same thing too!

Eve said to Adam 'Now my dear,
do you love only me?'
Adam replied 'I haven't got
a choice, that I can see!'

After the baby's christening
the father held his boy.
A lady guest came up to him
her face alight with joy!

She saw the baby in his arms
and gave a little 'coo',
and then she said 'If you don't mind,
I'd like a cuddle too!'

The father smiled at her request.
'Of course,' she heard him say.
'I'll put the baby down, and then
we'll have one straight away!'

SPORTING STORIES!

One sunny Sunday morning the vicar
was sick, or so he said.
He packed his clubs into his bag
and went to play golf instead.

He drove a great distance away
where nobody would see,
and on a country golf course
he stood on the first tee.

Just at that moment Saint Peter
said to God 'What will You do?
You will not let him get away
with missing church, will You?'

God shook his head, and then they watched
the vicar drive his ball,
and he was just about to play
his finest shot of all!

It took a moment for the vicar
to realise what he'd done.
It was the first time in his life
he'd had a hole in one!

Saint Peter said 'Some punishment!
A hole in one as well!'
 'Ah' God replied, 'but think on this.
Whoever can he tell?!'

A golfer said 'I'd move heaven and earth
if I could just improve!'
His partner said 'At least you're finding
it easy to make the earth move!'

LOVELINES!

She said 'He is a man of rare gifts!'
describing her husband Fred.
 'I can't remember when he last
gave me anything,' she said!

 'I hear young Susan's got married at last.
To a second lieutenant, they say.'
Her friend replied 'How did that happen?'
 'I believe the first one got away!'

He said 'My mother-in-law just vanished,
yesterday after tea!'
 'Have you described her to the police?'
 'I don't think that they'd believe me!'

He promised he'd mention his wife,
and when they read out his will
they found a note at the bottom
just saying 'Hello, there, Jill!'

She said 'My husband was a war baby.
When he was born one night
my parents took one look at him
and then began to fight!'

She said 'When I see a mirror
I always spend quite a while
admiring my flawless complexion
and watching my lovely smile.'

She turned to her husband and asked
 'Would you call that vanity?'
He said 'To be honest it sounds more
like imagination to me!'

CHILDREN SAY THE FUNNIEST THINGS!

Tommy and his little sister
were arguing one again.
'Why can't you both agree for once?'
asked mother, under strain!

Tommy answered 'That's not fair!
This time we do agree.
Both of us want the biggest slice
of chocolate cake for tea!'

Young Jimmy started trumpet lessons
and every time he blew
the family labrador would howl
and bark the whole way through!

Jimmy turned to his mum and said
 'That dog will have to go!
Surely there must be just one song
that Sandy doesn't know?!'

Young Sarah and her mother
went for a walk one day.
A lady stopped and said 'Wood Farm?
Can you please show me the way?'

The mother told her. As she went
young Sarah thoughtfully said
 'If people don't know where to go
they should stay at home instead!'

'If you eat your spinach, it will bring
colour to your cheeks, my lad.'
 'If I get green cheeks Mum' said Tim,
'I won't be very glad!'

COFFEE BREAK

The school secretary was finding out
a new pupil's situation.
  'Freddy' she asked, 'Can you tell me
your father's occupation?'

  'He's a conjurer, Miss' he told her.
She asked 'What's his favourite illusion?'
  'He saws up people in two, Miss.'
She blushed bright red in confusion!

  'Has he got any brothers and sisters?'
the secretary asked Freddy's mother.
She gave a wry smile, saying, 'two half sisters,
and he's also got one half brother!'

It was a hot day in the classroom.
The teacher said 'Ninety today!'
and then from the back 'Happy Birthday!'
young Jimmy was heard to say.

Young Bill's mother said 'You know the couple
that have come to live next door.
I had coffee with them this morning
and I'm getting to like them more.'

Their names are Derek and Janice Hills
and what's so funny, you see,
is that both Mr and Mrs Hills are
exactly the same age as me!'

Next week the teacher happened to read
an interesting story of Bill's.
In it, he wrote 'I've found that my mother
is just as old as the Hills!'

CHURCH CHUCKLES!

A lively member of the church
said 'Vicars, will you please pray
for My Young Son, particularly
this coming Saturday?'

The vicar did as he was asked,
then said 'How is your son?'
The man replied 'He's really great.
He won at 10 to 1?'

The doctor and the vicar one night
were beside a sick patient's bed.
The doctor and the vicar both
said 'poor old chap, he's dead!'

At that the man sat up in bed.
    'I'm still here!' he cried, distressed.
His wife said 'Lie down dear. The doctor
and the vicar know best!'

The vicar thought at Christmas time
that he would like to see
if children understood the meaning
of Christ's Nativity.

    'What difference would it make, children'
the vicar said to them
    'If Jesus Christ had not been born
that night at Bethlehem?'

Young Timothy put up his hand.
    'That's good' the vicar said,
until he heard the boy reply
    'You'd have another job instead!'

ANIMAL ANTICS!

A man locked himself out of his house
after having a drink one night.
He stood there for quite a while thinking
how he could get out of his plight.

The cat was inside, and he called out
  'Can you help me to get in now?'
There was a slight pause, then he heard
his cat replying 'Me? How?!'

He said 'My horse was going too fast,
and throwing me up and down.
I won't go on that roundabout
next time the fair's in town!'

The parrot was on the coal bunker
when the coalman arrived one day.
  'Put another bag in here'
he heard the parrot say!

The parrot said it again and again,
and had a great big laugh,
for in the end there were heaps of coal
lying all over the path!

The parrot hid when the owner
came home, for is mood was bad!
When he found that the cat had eaten
his kippers, he went really mad!

He threw the cat out, because he wasn't
the happiest of men!
The parrot asked the cat 'How many
bags did you order, then?!'

CHILDREN SAY THE FUNNINEST THINGS!

'When are you going to do your trick,
Grandma?' asked little Fred.
Looking bewildered, she asked 'What trick?'
'You can drink like a fish, Daddy said!'

'I hope I can't see you copying
Tommy's work, Jimmy' she cried.
'I certainly hope you can't, miss,
guiltily Jimmy replied!

'Now Jimmy, were the questions
in my test too hard for you?'
'No teacher, but I found each one
of the answers too hard to do!'

A conceited man at a party
was telling them all what he'd done.
'I've been to most countries in the world
and hunted in every one!'

The man was such an insufferable bore,
but one boy who had heard all his news
set everyone laughing, when he replied
'Why, whatever did you lose?!'

'My teacher asked me 'Will you have
brothers and sisters coming here?'
His mother said 'That's nice of her
to take such an interest, dear.'

'When she asked me if there were
any more children to come,
I told her I was an only child
and she said 'Thank goodness!', mum!'

LIFE'S LIKE THAT!

He wanted his house decorated
and asked some firms to quote.
One estimate was so much less
he thought 'They'll have my vote!'

He saw the man in charge who said
'Our work is second to none!
We'll come along to decorate
as soon as this job's done.'

'I like to supervise my staff
and keep them on the go.'
He kept on calling 'Green side up
to people down below.

'Why have you shouted 'Green side up'
a dozen times or more?'
'That's technical information' he said.
'They're laying a lawn next door!'

'Can I try on that dress in the window?'
She heard the assistant refuse.
'There's a changing room inside the store
we prefer all our shoppers to use!'

He was given a comb
but he had a bald head.
'I'll never part with it'
the bald man said!

'I'm too tired to do my homework, Mum!'
'Hard work never killed anyone.'
' But I don't want to be the first'
replied her lazy son!

CHILDRENS PRAYERS

'Dear God' young Susan prayed one night,
'Please tell me how I began.
I hope You can explain it better
than both my parents can!'

'I like Your Bible' young Timothy said.
'It's the best book I've read for years,
but what I'd like to ask You is
where did You get all Your ideas?!'

'Do you think boys are better than girls?'
young Angela asked God in prayer.
'I know that You are one, but can
You please try to be fair!'

Douglas was rather a thoughtful lad,
although he was young and small.
'What are colds for?' he asked God one night.
'They don't seem much use at all!'

Tom prayed to God 'I find Christmas
comes too late in the year for me.
I think it's so hard to be good
for nearly a year, You see!'

'Dear God, I was just wondering'
one night in her prayers said young Pat,
'did You mean to make a giraffe
with such a long neck as that?!'

'Dear God' young Sarah prayed one night.
'This worries me quite a lot.
Instead of letting people die,
why don't You keep the ones You've got?!'

CHURCH CHUCKLES!

When they arrived at the local church
the congregation were shocked.
Instead of the normal welcome, they found
the doors were bolted and locked.

No service, but then they saw on the door
a note from the vicar instead.
   'You've all been coming long enough.
Now do what I've told you' it read!

He spent six months inside a jail
because he had offended.
For several hours each day they gave
him mail bags to be mended.

The vicar watched and said 'I see
that you are busy sewing.'
The prisoner replied 'In truth
I'm reaping what I'm owing!'

   'I never go to church, vicar'
a woman said one day.
   'I think it's just a waste of time,
and I'm none the worse, I'd say.'

The vicar told me, adding that
he'd answered when he met her.
   'You might be none the worse, my dear,
but are you any better?!'

The vicar said 'we have installed
another font, dear friends.
This is good news, for babies can
be baptised at both ends!'

MOTORING MADNESS!

A lorry containing tons of glue
has just spilt its heavy load.
Motorists travelling on that route
should stick to the side of the road!

She told her husband 'I don't think
your driving's as good as mine.
I got back to my car and found
a note saying 'Parking Fine'!

A man was walking down a road,
and hadn't got too far
when he could hear the squeal of brakes
and see a speeding car.

The sight of it was quite enough
to set his nerves on edge,
and in his panic then he threw
himself into a hedge!

A little frightened and annoyed
　'Road hog!' the pedestrian cried.
The driver wound his window down.
　'Hedgehog' the man replied!

　'This car has had one careful owner'
the garage salesman said.
　'It's covered with dents and scratches!'
replied my Uncle Fred.

　'That is quite true' the salesman said.
　'One owner took great care.
Unfortunately the other ones
left it in disrepair!'

LOVELINES!

'Shall I marry a girl who can take a joke?'
he asked his father one day.
'Son, that's the only kind you'll get'
his father was heard to say!'

Her wedding day was coming up
with a million things to do.
She chatted with her mother, saying
  'You will help, mum, won't you?'

  'I want the day to be as perfect
as it can possibly be.
I just don't want a single thing
to be missed out, you see.'

  'I'm determined not to overlook
the most unimportant detail!'
Her mother said 'I'll make sure dear
that the bridegroom's there, without fail!'

She told the vicar 'I want a divorce.
I've tried to be a good wife.'
The vicar said 'When you were wed
you promised it was for life!'

She said 'I understand all that,
but sadly it appears
that my poor husband hasn't shown
any life at all for years!'

  'My daughter wanted a simple wedding'
her father said, full of gloom.
  'She got exactly what she wanted,
starting with the groom!'

CHILDREN SAY THE FUNNIEST THINGS!

A boy came home from school one day
and said 'I helped a lot.
The teacher asked me for answers
each time that she forgot!'

A boy went off to Sunday School,
and as a special treat
he took two coins, one to give in,
and one to buy some sweets.

He ran along the road, but tripped,
and getting up again
he saw that one of his two coins
had fallen down a drain.

The boy looked up to Heaven and
paused before moving on,
then said 'I'm really sorry God
but Your coin has just gone!'

'Now tell me Jimmy, is the world
quite flat or it is round?'
' My Mum says it's crooked, Miss.
At least that's what she's found!'

In a Church Exam one question read
  'What does a Bishop do?'
One boy wrote 'Moves across the board,
and takes other pieces too!'

'Why do folk call me a Christian?'
a pompous man asked a small boy.
  'I think it's because they don't know you'
the young lad replied with great joy!

MEDICAL MATTERS!

A men went off to the doctor's.
'I'm losing my memory' he cried.
The doctor asked 'When did you notice?'
'Notice what?' the patient replied!

A young man who was keen once joined
the Ambulance Brigade.
He went each week and sought a chance
to practise his first aid.

He saw a large crowd in the street,
with someone lying there.
The opportunity had come
for him to tend and care.

He saw an old man bending down
and boldly took his place.
  'Now please stand back, if you don't mind.
I need a bit of space.'

The old man duly moved aside,
then said sarcastically
  'I'm just a doctor, but I don't
suppose that you need me!'

  'Do you know, every morning, Doctor
I find myself under the bed!'
  'My friend, you must be a little
potty,' the doctor said!

The hospital, where her husband died
sent a note of consolation.
She answered, thanking the nurses and doctors
for their kind co-operation!'

COFFEE BREAK

'Now, how do you spell 'blancmange'?'
the dinner lady asked with a frown.
She was doing the children's lunches,
and writing the menu down.

'I haven't a clue!' her assistant said.
'My dear, if you take my advice,
just leave it off the menu today.
I'll open some tins of rice!'

'Jimmy, I think your work has improved.
I can only find ten mistakes here.'
Jimmy looked pleased, till the teacher said
  'Now we'll look at the second line, dear!'

She had four large scoops of ice cream
on two slices of apple pie.
It was covered with lashings of raspberry sauce
and chopped nuts were piled on high!

She was asked 'Would you like a cherry on top?'
and replied, 'No, I don't think I'll try it.
To be quite honest, I'm trying hard
to keep to a brand new diet!'

He was trying to cross the channel
on a plank, but found it tough.
He gave up, because he couldn't find
a plank that was long enough!

He said 'I'm very sorry to hear
that your mother-in-law has died.
What was the complaint?' 'Well, up to now
we've not had one' he replied!

CHURCH CHUCKLES!

The vicar dipped his hands in the font
and smiled at the folk gathered there,
then he rolled up both his sleeves and said
 'The baby is in here somewhere!'

The vicar was quite progressive
and eager to rearrange,
but found that his congregation
were quite resistant to change.

He wanted to move the piano,
but mindful of everyone's fears
he moved it just one inch a week
for nearly seven years!

Three vicars on a walk one day
saw a river deep and wide.
The first one boldly walked across
and reached the other side!

The second vicar followed him
and reached the far side too.
The third one gasped, but told himself
 'It can't be hard to do!'

He started out, but right away
the poor chap had to swim!
The first two vicars had a laugh,
then they confessed to him.

When he found out the truth, you never
heard some moans and groans!
You see, the first two vicars crossed
by using stepping stones!

ANIMAL ANTICS!

A man had four penguins in his car
and a policeman came along.
The policeman said 'Excuse me, sir.
What you're doing is quite wrong.'

  'The penguins shouldn't be in here!
Now you know what to do.
I think that you should take them
immediately to the zoo!'

The following day, the policeman
saw the penguins in the car.
The driver said 'They liked the zoo.
We're off to the cinema!'

Jimmy was asked to name an animal
from Australia, if he could.
He replied 'A kangaroo, miss!'
The teacher said 'That's good!'

  'Now, can you name another one?
There's a prize if you get two.'
Jimmy thought for a moment, then he said
  'Another kangaroo!'

  'What family does the crocodile
belong to?' she asked one day.
  'Nobody here has got one, Miss,'
young Jimmy was heard to say!'

  'Now children, can you name three members
that come from the cat family?'
  'Daddy, Mummy and Baby cat, Miss'
replied little Emily!

CHILDREN SAY THE FUNNIEST THINGS!

Young Sally asked 'Does Father Christmas
bring the presents I need?'
Her mother smiled, and answered her
'Yes, that is true indeed.'

Then Sally asked her mother
'Mummy, did the stork bring me?'
Her mother answered, quite relieved
'That's right dear. Time for tea!'

But Sally hadn't finished yet!
'I heard my teacher say
that God provides our clothes and all
we need to eat each day.'

The mother told her little girl
'Yes dear, that's very true.'
Young Sally thought, then said 'But Mummy
what does Daddy do?'

'Do you know how much an airmail letter
to Washington costs, young Fred?'
'I wouldn't bother to send one, Miss,
because I've heard that he's dead!'

'Why is your little brother crying?'
she asked her young son Tim.
'Because I've got my piece of cake
and won't give it to him.'

'Well, what about his piece of cake?
I gave them both to you.'
'Well, actually,' young Tim replied
'he cried when I ate that, too!'

LIFE'S LIKE THAT!

The couple had a theatre trip,
but in a while she found
her husband got quite restless, and
began peering around.

He settled for a while, and then
he searched around once more.
He nudged his wife, and said to her
  'My toffee's on the floor!'

She really got fed up with him!
  'Just leave the toffee, dear.'
He said 'My teeth are stuck to it!
It must be somewhere here!'

  'Here's your first class stamp, Madam'
the post office counter clerk said.
She asked 'Do I stick it on myself?'
  'We prefer them on the envelope instead!'

Four men were celebrating
in a Public House one night.
They looked and saw there was only
one other man in sight.

They asked him 'Do you often come
and sit here on your own?'
When he said 'Yes' they said 'Join us,
and you won't be alone.'

  'What will you have to drink?' he said.
  'A double brandy then.'
  'No wonder he is on his own!
said one of the four men!

CHURCH CHUCKLES!

After weeks of investigation
and some considerable delay
death watch beetle has been confirmed
in Durham Cathedral today.

The Bishop of Durham has duly
followed the church's advice,
and he has also confirmed three bates,
two spiders and three small mice!

Moses wore the very first wig.
Of that I have no doubt.
Sometimes he was seen with Aaron,
and sometimes seen without!

It's sad to think the real truth
of Christmas is now missed.
I saw a lady in a shop
checking her Christmas card list.

  'My husband likes religious cards,
so I'll buy a box of these,
but have you got in stock something
a little more Christmassy, please?!'

The Post Office committee said
  'The item that comes next
is whether Christmas mail should
be stamped with bible texts?'

One member said 'I've got a text
I think we should discuss.
Let's stamp upon each envelope
  'May God deliver us!'

LOVELINES!

The absent minded professor's wife
entered his study to say
  'Do you know, you asked me to marry you
thirty years ago today?!'

The professor looked up from his work.
  'Don't tell me. Let me guess.
What did you reply to that?
Did you say 'No' or 'Yes'?!'

A daughter told her mother once
  'I've got a new boy friend!'
Her mother asked 'Is he someone
on whom you can depend?'

  'Oh yes' her daughter said at once.
  'He's such a lovely bloke.
He doesn't go out very much,
and doesn't drink or smoke.'

  'He always dressed smartly,
and he cooks as well as you.
His children are so well behaved.
His wife is quite nice too!'

He said 'Our son is the image of me!'
She said, feeling rather unkind.
  'As long as the boy is healthy
I don't think that I really mind!'

The policeman said 'Your wife fell out
of your car five miles ago!'
  'Well, that's a relief!' the husband said.
  'I thought I'd gone deaf, you know!'

CHILDREN SAY THE FUNNIEST THINGS!

A man was cycling along,
not taking the greatest care.
He braked, and fell off in the road,
his arms and legs everywhere.

A little girl walked by, and said
'I sympathise with you.
My Daddy has just taken off
my stabilizers too!'

'What does the story of Jonah
and the whale teach us, young Fred?'
'It shows us Miss, that you just can't keep
a good man down' he said.

'When you've finished your exams,
what are you going to be?'
'Probably a pensioner!'
replied young Timothy.

Three Boy Scouts told their leader
they had done their day's good deed.
'We saw a little old lady,
and we helped her in her need.'

'We helped her get across the road,'
'Are you sure it took all three
to help just one old lady?'
he asked suspiciously.

At first the boys were silent,
then the smallest one said 'No.
I asked the other two to help
as she didn't want to go!'

LIFE'S LIKE THAT!

One lady said 'I want my children
to have all I couldn't afford,
and then I can move in with them
and enjoy my free bed and board!'

'Are you trying to be awkward?'
'No sir' young Jimmy replied.
'Well, you're doing quite well, without trying'
the poor harassed schoolmaster sighed!

A hungry weary tramp called at
the George and Dragon one night.
The innkeeper's wife gazed haughtily
and said 'You look a sight!'

He asked her 'Can you spare some food?'
She cried 'Tramps don't get fed!'
The tramp thought 'This must be the dragon!
May I speak to George?' he said!

He applied for a job as a prison warden.
Said the governor 'It's tough here, you know.'
The applicant said 'If they don't behave,
I shall just tell each one 'Out you go!'

A drunk was staggering along
when a lamppost got in his way!
He bumped into another one
and thought 'This isn't my day!'

It happened a third time, and he said
 'I'd better sit down here,
and wait till all these people pass
when the pavement will be clear!'

CHURCH CHUCKLES!

The vicar preached about the prophets
quite slowly, one by one.
One dear old soul got really bored
and thought 'It's not much fun!'

'Where shall I put Isaiah?' he asked.
She called out 'I don't care.
I'm going home for dinner, so
he's welcome to my chair!'

They held their school nativity,
their faces all aglow.
Five children were to hold up cards
that said the word 'Hello'.

Unfortunately, I have to say
things didn't go too well.
The last child came in first, and so
the cards then read 'O Hell!'

The church ladies held an evening
when the village hall was hired.
They had to bring something along
that they no longer required.

They called it a 'Swap Social'.
It was a successful 'do'.
Apparently many ladies chose
to bring their husbands too!

The vicar, praying for the sick
said 'We must pray for Win.
Her teeth have just been taken out,
and a new gas stove put in!'

CHILDREN SAY THE FUNNIEST THINGS!

She said to Rachel 'We're going to lunch
with Aunty Sue and Uncle Dave.
Always say 'please' and 'thank you',
and be polite and behave!'

Lunch came. Aunty Sue said to Rachel
 'Would you like me to cut your meat?'
 'No thank you' said Rachel. 'Sometimes at home
it's as tough as this to eat!'

'Mum, you told me to fill the salt cellar,
but when will it be time to stop?
I'm having a lot of trouble getting
the salt through the holes in the top!'

'Mum, Jimmy broke a pane of glass
in the greenhouse just today.
I threw a ball at him, and he ducked,
trying to get out of the way!'

Sarah looked at her Aunt Georgina,
as she started to eat her main course.
 'When are you putting your nosebag on?
Daddy says you eat like a horse!'

She said 'Jimmy, you mustn't tell lies.
Do you know, when I was small
I was a really good little girl
and didn't tell lies at all!'

Young Jimmy looked in disbelief
then said 'straight from the heart
 'I promise I will try to be good,
but Mum, when did you start?!'

LIFE'S LIKE THAT!

We planned our holiday last year
and sought local advice.
We mentioned weather, and they said
   'Last week we had rain twice.'

We said 'That's really not too bad!'
They said 'It's pretty poor.
Firstly it rained for three days
then it rained for four days more!'

She had a ten pound note in one year,
and ten in the other one.
   'Mrs Brown is ten pounds in arrears'
explained the landlord's son!

She said 'We're so proud of our son
in every single way.
He went to University,
but it was shut that day!'

She seemed quite surrounded by children!
   'Are all of them yours?' I cried.
She wearily said 'I'm afraid so.
I've three boys and six girls' she replied.

Now maths is not really my strong point,
but 'That's nine altogether' I said.
   'That's not right' the mother insisted
   'We had then one at a time instead!'

We arrived as the train was pulling out.
The porter said 'Well sir, that's tough!
Have you missed the train?' The man replied
   'I didn't know it well enough!'

CHURCH CHUCKLES!

A vicar took the funeral
of one of his congregation.
He praised the man so highly
and was full of admiration.

He spoke of all his virtues, and
how much he was respected.
So much in fact, that his widow
was adversely affected.

She turned in disbelief towards
her son, and said 'I'd rather
the vicar said something I thought
was true about your father!'

He went to a shop to buy the Church Times.
The shopkeeper said with regret
  'It hasn't come in. Some of the other
comics have not arrived yet!'

The vicar gave a powerful talk
on 'Death' and 'Judgement' one day.
He said 'All those in this parish
will die and be judged God's way.'

A man in the front row sat laughing.
Said the vicar 'It's not funny to me!'
  'But,' said the man in the front row
  'I don't live in this parish, you see!'

The Church magazine said that Rev Brown
was elected as vicar today.
  'We could not get a better man'
the notice went on to say!

ANIMAL ANTICS!

He told his friend 'I've bought a pig!'
His friend said 'I've heard it all!
Wherever will you keep the thing?
Your garden's much too small!'

'I know all that, and I have thought
the matter out' he said.
'I have decided that I'll keep
it underneath my bed!'

'What, keep the pig in your bedroom?
It's bound to smell a bit!'
'I've thought that out as well' he said
'It will soon get used to it!'

They'd gone to a very posh restaurant
for little Fred's birthday treat.
His father thought it a shame to leave
all the food they couldn't eat.

'Could we have a bag of leftovers
to give to our dog?' he said.
'Wow Dad, that's wonderful news.
Are we getting a dog?' asked Fred.

Young Jimmy cried 'My puppy's gone.
He must have run away!'
His father said 'Don't worry, son.
I'll write some notes today.'

'I'll pin them up around the town.
He's quite a special breed.'
Young Jimmy said 'He might be, Dad,
but he hasn't yet learned to read!'

SPORTING STORIES!

The vicar was useless at golf,
although he tried quite hard.
He was ashamed to mark his score
so never took a card.

One day his play was just the same.
He found the sand and trees,
then in despair the vicar knelt
and prayed upon his knees.

'Dear Lord' he said 'give me one chance
to show what I can do!'
He stood upon the next tee, and
his ball just simply flew!

Up, up it soared, and then he saw
exactly what he'd done.
The ball went down the cup. The vicar
had a hole in one!'

His prayer was answered, but his conscience
still caused him to groan.
'Thank You' he said 'but how I wish
I'd done it on my own!'

The captain had missed a penalty.
'I could kick myself' he cried!
The manager just smiled at him.
' You'd probably miss' he replied!

The goalkeeper let about ten goals in!
He said that he'd just caught a cold.
'We're all very glad you can catch something!'
the poor goalkeeper was told!

LOVELINES!

He told his wife 'Your mother's got
tremendous staying power!
In fact each time she comes, she stays
hour after hour after hour!'

He telephoned his girlfriend to ask
  'Will you marry me, Denise?'
  'Of course I will my dear' she said.
  'Who is that calling, please?'

'Boys whisper that they love me!'
she told a friend, feeling proud.
Her friend replied 'Quite obviously,
they wouldn't admit it out loud!'

She said 'I am getting married!'
  'That's wonderful news!' her friend said,
  'but you always said men were stupid,
and that you'd never get wed.'

  'That's perfectly true' the girl answered,
but sometimes thing happen, you see,
and now I have finally found one
who's willing to marry me!'

  'I've got some super news' she said.
  'I'm getting engaged, Dad!'
Her father said 'Can you tell me
some more about the lad?'

  'Has he got money put aside,
and decent prospects too?'
His daughter said 'You know, he asked
the same things about you!'

CHILDREN SAY THE FUNNIEST THINGS!

Young Richard went to church with his Aunt
for the first time, when he was three.
He came home smiling, and he said
I had a nice time, Mummy.'

'Some men brought round a great big plate
with lots of money piled high.
but I told them that I didn't want any.
I'm a good boy, Mummy, aren't I?'

One afternoon, while having tea
she heard her young son Ben
say 'Mummy, my teacher's taught me
how to count up to ten!'

He recited proudly, and she said
'You are a clever thing!'
Now do you know what comes next?'
He answered 'Jack', 'Queen', 'King'!'

A little boy down at the seaside
was crying alone on the sand.
An elderly lady took pity
and hurried to take the child's hand.

'I want my Mummy' the little lad cried.
The lady said 'Come with me dear.
I'll get you an ice cream, and then I'm sure
we'll find that your mummy is near.'

She bought him an ice cream, then told him
'We'll look for her now,' but the lad
said 'Don't bother. I know where she is.
It's the third free ice cream that I've had!'

COFFEE BREAK

A blacksmith went to court one day.
The judge said 'Now, my good man
I think I shall find you guilty
of forging, if I can!'

'Are you the waiter who took my order?
It's been so long since the evening began
that somehow my wife and I both expected
to see a much older man!'

A dry cleaner was called for jury service.
He said 'I find that distressing!
I'd like to be excused if I may
as my business is always pressing!'

'My husband's career is in ruins!' she cried.
Her friend said 'That is so sad.'
She said 'He's an archaeologist,
so it's really not that bad!'

The couple next door haven't spoken
to each other for three whole years!
They haven't rowed, but they just can't think
of something to say, it appears!

'What is your height and position?'
they radioed to Pete.
He answered 'I'm about six feet tall
and I'm in the pilot's seat!'

He said 'I'm not going in that plane.
It's far too old' he cried.
'Just look at it! It's even got
a toilet and washroom outside!'

MEDICAL MATTERS!

A lady who suffered from confusion
went to the doctor's one day.
She had such a terrible memory
she forgot everything straight away!

   'Doctor Jones will see you now, Madam.'
   'Which doctor?' the lady replied.
   'Oh no' the receptionist answered.
   'You'll find that he's well qualified!'

   'I need something to keep my stomach in.'
The doctor said 'I can help you.'
He sent his assistant around the back
and asked 'Will a wheelbarrow do?!'

   'You have acute appendicitis,
Mrs Brown' the young doctor said.
She replied 'I came to be examined,
not to be admired instead!'

He phoned up the doctor one night and said
   'Doctor, I really need you.
My mother-in-law is at death's door.
Can you help to pull her through?!'

   'Doctor, I'm feeling better today,
but my breathing still troubles me'
   'Perhap's I can put a stop to that'
the doctor said thoughtfully!

   'Now, how do you feel today, my dear?'
the doctor asked young Sue.
She answered 'With my hands, doctor,
that way that I usually do!'

CHURCH CHUCKLES!

A vicar said to a young father
'I hear God's brought twin sons to you!'
The young father said 'And God knows where
their school fees are coming from too!'

'I think I shall marry a doctor,
and be ill for nothing' she said.
Her friend said 'I'll marry a vicar,
and be good for nothing instead!'

The new vicar preached his first sermon.
His churchwarden was sick and away.
They met up, and he told the vicar
 'I'm sorry I missed last Sunday.'

'You didn't miss much' said the vicar.
with a show of extreme modesty.
The churchwarden smiled, and then answered
 'That's what the others told me!'

The Church Fellowship went on an outing
to a church several hundred years old.
 'There's a plaque to a brave young man who died
at Waterloo,' the vicar was told.

Entering into the spirit of things,
with great interest the vicar replied
 'You've just been along to read it, my friend.
Does it say on which platform he died?'

Our organist is wonderful.
He plays until he drops.
My friend was so impressed, and said
 'He pulls out all the stops!'

SOMETHING TO THINK ABOUT!

The vicar went off to a meeting.
His wife said 'Drive carefully, please do.
Not only cars can be recalled
by their maker, but those driving them too!'

Grandad was deaf, but he would go
to church each week to praise.
His Grandson said 'Why go, when you
can't hear what the vicar says?'

His Grandad thought a while, and then
replied, while his face shone
  'You see, my lad, I want the world
to know whose side I'm on!'

I think a famous man once wrote
  'The best is yet to come.
I've been and fallen in the pond.
Just tell that to my Mum!'

My friend is always doing things for folk.
Right now he's not overjoyed.
He's come to learn that a friend in need
is often someone to avoid!

The Union of Spiritualist Mediums
had a dance, and the haunting refrain
they chose for the last waltz of the evening
was of course 'I'll see you again!'

You know, money does talk
in all situations,
and where there is a will
there are always relations!

CHILDREN SAY THE FUNNIEST THINGS!

She went to see Father Christmas
as a special treat last year.
He smiled at her, and then he asked
'How old are you, my dear?'

'I'm three' she told him proudly.
'How nice! When were you three?'
'On my last birthday' she replied,
a little impatiently.

Rachel had a baby brother named Ben,
and though she was only four,
her mother thought she'd be pleased to know
that she was expecting once more.

'Now Rachel, how would you like to have
another baby sister or brother?'
After a little pause for thought
young Rachel answered her mother.

'I know that he's very naughty, Mummy,
and he's really quite a trial,
but I think we should keep our Ben,
because we've had him a good while!'

Young Sally said 'When I'm grown up
I shall marry Mike or Ted!'
'You'll have to make your mind up, dear,'
her mother gently said.

She thought, then said 'I've decided
that I shall marry Mike.'
When her mother asked why, she answered
'He's got a better bike!'

LIFE'S LIKE THAT!

He went to the station to buy a ticket.
'Change at Kings Cross' the clerk said.
The passenger answered 'If you don't mind
I would like my change here instead!'

'I've not got a big head, have I?'
a boy asked his mother one day.
His mother consoled him and told him
'Don't listen to all that they say.'

'Now, please get me a bag of potatoes.
Don't be long, there's a good chap.
There's no need to take a shopping bag.
You can carry them home in your cap!'

A wife thought she heard a prowler
in the middle of the night.
She told her husband 'Creep downstairs,
and don't switch on the light.'

'Sneak up on him before he knows
that you are even near.'
Her husband put on his dressing gown
and said to his wife 'Yes dear.'

'If it's not too much trouble' she added,
as he reached the bedroom door,
'Can you bring me a glass of water
when you come back upstairs once more?!'

The notice said 'Apples, 60 pence a pound'.
The caterpillar had to look twice,
then said to his friend 'Aren't houses today
such an exorbitant price?!'

LOVELINES!

He said 'I hear your wife's rather large.'
The husband replied 'I should say.
When I carried her over the threshold,
I had to make two trips that day!'

At a dance she saw a young man
approach across the floor.
He looked a real handsome chap.
She felt her spirits soar!

He asked her 'Are you going to dance?'
  'Yes,' shyly she replied.
  'That's good' he said. 'I'll have your chair
and watch you from the side!'

'My husband just simply adores me!
He eats out of my hand' she said.
Her friend said 'It sounds unhygienic.
We use a dishwasher instead!'

He told his girlfriend 'Our dog's like
one of the family.'
She saw the funny side of that!
  'Which one?' she asked cheekily!

She asked 'Should our young son take
up the piano as a career?'
Her husband replied 'He should put down
the lid as a favour, my dear!'

  'I thought I'd found my Mr Right
the day that we were wed.
I didn't know his first name
was 'Always' though' she said!

ANIMAL ANTICS!

While fishing off the Florida coast
a tourist capsized one day.
He clung on to the upturned boat
as sharks had been seen that way.

He called to a beachcomber on the shore
and told him of his fears.
   'Don't worry, pal' the beachcomber cried.
   'We've not had sharks for years!'

So, feeling safe, he left the boat
and swam towards the shore.
About halfway, he called 'I'm glad
you don't have sharks any more!'

   'Now, how did you get rid of them?'
   'We did nothing' came the call.
   'We think the alligators around
here must have got them all!'

'Giraffes find it hard to apologise'
young Jimmy explained to me.
He told me 'It takes them such a while
to swallow their pride, you see!'

A farmer reared chickens with four legs,
and locals soon spread the word!
The radio and television
stations quite quickly heard.

One of the reporters said hungrily
   'They're tasty, I'm willing to bet!'
The farmer replied 'Well, actually
I haven't caught one of them yet!'

CHURCH CHUCKLES!

'The church is full of hypocrites!'
he said, when the vicar came to call.
'Why don't you join us?' the vicar replied,
for one more won't harm us t all!'

A new but keen church member looked
at the finances with some surprise.
He noticed an item for five hundred pounds
marked down as 'pulpit supplies.'

Not knowing the cost was for preachers
he said 'It seems terribly dear,'
then went to the pulpit and said 'There's just
a glass of water in here!'

Said the vicar to the curate
  'I think I've got a hunch!
I wonder if my sermons are too long
for those who want their lunch?'

The curate told the vicar
  'You do keep us rather late.
Perhaps the hunch though can be cured
if you just stand up straight!'

Two nuns drove in their mini car.
One parked while her friend shopped,
then couldn't find the car again.
A friendly vicar stopped.

She asked the vicar 'Have you seen
a nun in a red mini, please?'
The vicar said 'I didn't know
that nuns wore clothes like these!'

MOTORING MADNESS!

The vicar was driving one afternoon,
and hadn't got very far,
when a sports car driver, going too fast
drove into his much loved car!

The vicar remembered his status in life,
but nevertheless was quite cross.
  'I really can't fathom you young fellows out'
the vicar said, quite at a loss!

  'I'm so sorry vicar' the young man replied.
  'I just didn't see you somehow.'
He took out a flask of whisky and said
  'Have a drink. This will calm your nerves now.'

'I don't normally drink' the vicar replied,
'but I'd still like to drink your good health.'
He drank quite a generous portion, then said
  'Won't you have some whisky yourself?'

'Oh no,' said the young man, 'I make it a rule
never to drink when I drive.
Let's just sit here for a moment or two
and wait for the police to arrive!'

A young man caught for speeding
was asked to give his name.
He said 'Lots of others do it.
Do you treat them all the same?'

The policeman quickly answered him
  'Do you go fishing, son?'
When he said 'Yes,' the policeman asked
  'Well, do you catch each one?'

CHILDREN SAY THE FUNNIEST THINGS!

A mum went to the local chip shop
and took her young daughter Sue.
They waited very patiently,
having joined a very long queue.

The door of the shop opened suddenly
and a middle aged hippy walked in.
He had long wavy blonde hair, and a beard,
and his face had the loveliest grin.

He was wearing a canvas cloak, and had
simple sandals on his feet.
Little Sue's face was lit up with joy.
It had made her day so complete.

She grabbed her mother's arm, and stared
as wide eyed as she could be.
  'To think that Jesus has come inside
our fish and chip shop, mummy!'

Timothy had a baby sister
but wasn't too full of joy!
He'd told his parents countless times
that he wanted a little boy!

One day the baby was crying,
and Tim's mother hurriedly came.
She had a sneaking feeling
that someone was to blame!

  'Do you know why she's crying?'
she asked young Timothy.
  'Maybe somebody pinched her'
he answered guiltily!

COFFEE BREAK

Two drunks were staggering down the road.
One said 'My friend, I see
we must have walked by chance into
the local cemetery!'

He said 'I've found a gravestone here.'
His friend said 'What a shame!
I know we've had a drink or two
but can you read the name?'

The first drunk knelt upon the ground.
With difficulty he read,
then turning to the other drunk
   'His name is Miles' he said.

His friend asked 'Is there any more?'
He said 'I can't yet tell.'
then after quite a time, added
   'It's got '200 to London' as well!'

The football coach told one of his boys
   'My lad, do you agree
that we shouldn't lose our temper
and shout at the referee?'

'We shouldn't throw things on the pitch,
for football's a game to enjoy.
Now do you understand all that?'
   'Yes sir,' replied the boy.

   'You are a very sensible lad.
Your attitude is grand.
I only wish your father
could also understand!'

THE BISHOP AND THE CHAUFFEUR

A certain Bishop preached the same
sermon again and again.
His chauffeur, who had heard each one
decided to complain.

'Why don't you write another one?'
'All right' the Bishop said,
'If you know it so well, next time
you preach it then instead!'

The chauffeur really thought that was
a wonderful idea.
The bishop donned the driver's coat
and lent him all his gear.

The chauffeur was word perfect as
he preached to many folk.
The congregation sat in awe
and listened as he spoke.

He grew in confidence, and as
his sermon reached its end
the bogus bishop chose to ask
  'Now, any questions, friends?'

He'd gone too far of course, and things
did not quite go as planned.
Somebody asked a question he
didn't even understand!

But then he brightened as he saw
the bishop near his side.
  'Even my chauffeur can tell you
the answer to that' he replied!

CHURCH CHUCKLES!

The vicar looked out of his window
and saw an old tramp kneeling down.
  'Now what are you doing, my good man?'
the vicar called out, with a frown.

'I'm so hungry, I'm eating the grass
on your front lawn' the old vagrant cried.
  'If you go round the back, you will find
that it's longer' the vicar replied!

A vicar on a bus, once saw
a man, who smelled of beer.
He asked the bus conductor
  'Are drunks allowed in here?'

The bus conductor shook his head.
  'No, that will never do,
but if you sit quite still, old chap,
no one will notice you!'

They've overhauled the organ, and
Mrs Brown caused celebrations,
when leaving her feet on the pedals
she changed her combinations!

The vicar went to hospital
to pray for one dear soul.
He prayed 'Lord, be with Mrs Smith.
Heal her, and make her whole.'

He felt a tug upon his sleeve,
  'Excuse me. Call me Vi.
My married name is not the one
that God will know me by!'

MEDICAL MATTERS!

'How would you cope with a drink problem?'
he asked the doctor one day.
The doctor considered the question, then said
'With a corkscrew, I would say!'

'People who cough very loudly
never go to the doctor's' he said
'I know because I always hear them
They go to the theatre instead!'

'They both keep biting nails'
she told the doctor, about her sons.
'My dear, that is quite common.'
'Not three inch rusty ones!'

'My husband's mind is straying.'
Said the doctor 'Leave things as they are.
I know your husband really well.
I'm certain it won't go too far!'

'Doctor, my tongue keeps sticking out!
What is it? Do you know?'
'If you could lick these stamps for me,
I'd be grateful, before you go!'

'If I take these little blue pills, doctor,
will I get better for sure?'
'Look at this way' the doctor said,
nobody's come back for more!'

'Now how do I stand, Doctor?'
asked an elderly man one day.
'That's exactly what puzzles me'
said the doctor, straight away!

LOVELINES!

He said 'My eldest sister fell
in love at second sight.
She didn't know how rich he was
when she met him the first night!'

A husband told his friend 'My wife
is really very dear.
She costs me a small fortune
each day of every year!'

'And is this your most charming wife?'
asked an overseas guest one day.
   'She's the only one I've got' he replied,
   'so it's rather hard to say!'

'We're really never on speaking terms'
a husband said to me,
   'but I'm on very good listening terms'
he added, ruefully!

   'She said she'd go through anything
for me' a husband sighed.
   'She's only managed to go through
my bank account' he cried!

Quite nervously he said 'I've come
to ask for your daughter's hand.'
   'You'll have to take the rest as well
young man, you understand!'

He asked 'If we ever got married,
could you live on my income, my dear?'
She answered 'I could, but that wouldn't
leave much at all for you, I fear!'

CHILDREN SAY THE FUNNIEST THINGS!

When Sarah was a baby, her Mum
got very few cuddles each day,
yet when she was three, she hugged her
in such an affectionate way!

Her mother said 'Now you are older
you're happy to cuddle me!'
Young Sarah said 'Now I am bigger
I know you much better, Mummy!'

Young Jimmy said 'I'll help you Mum
to sweep around the room.'
Surprised, but keen to encourage,
she handed him the broom.

A little later he called out,
and left her rather glum,
by saying 'I don't know which corner
to sweep it all into, Mum!'

The school had their Harvest Festival
and the gifts were all brought in.
The teacher talked about the loaves
and fishes to begin.

She told the children 'Now, although
we haven't any fish here,
we must remember that God provides
them every day of the year.'

There was a silence in the hall
and then a young boy named Chris
said 'Perhaps you didn't see I brought
a tin of salmon, Miss!'

LIFE'S LIKE THAT!

A tramp walked up to a passer-by.
'Have you got a bed for the night?'
'No, I haven't' the passer-by replied,
appalled to see such a sight.

'Have you got a pound for a meal?' he asked.
The passer-by shook his head.
'How about twenty pence for a cup of tea?'
'No, I haven't' the passer-by said.

The tramp looked at him, and then told him
'My, you're certainly in a jam.
You'd better have my mouth organ, for
you're even worse off than I am!'

A lady was playing Bingo,
but finding it terribly hard,
for the gentleman sitting beside her
kept trying to mark off her card.

'Why don't you check your own numbers?'
the lady eventually sighed.
'I've already filled my own card up'
the gentleman sadly replied!

'He's known as an after dinner speaker'
a dear lady I know, told me.
'Each time he speaks to a woman,
he's after a dinner, you see!'

Charlie was nervous on his first flight.
'Do planes often crash?' he enquired.
'We usually find that they only crash once'
said the new stewardess they'd just hired!

CHURCH CHUCKLES!

A young man was in the confessional.
'Can you help me, Father, please?'
'The Lord is merciful, my son.
Now tell me, what sins are these?'

'Can stealing three times be forgiven?'
'Yes, by God alone, my son,
but can you tell me while you're here
exactly what you've done?'

The petty thief replied, 'I stole
some money yesterday.
Today I visited a house
and took some cash away.'

'I'm sure the Lord God will forgive
the two sins that I've heard,
but you said three?' The thief replied
'Tomorrow will be the third!'

'You weren't in church last week, Jimmy.
I hear you played football instead.'
'That's not true, vicar. I've got three fish
to prove it' young Jimmy said!

The churchwarden asked the verger
'How did the wedding go?'
'Not too well' the verger replied.
'It's the vicar's squint, you know!'

'He married the groom to the best man
and kissed a bouquet of flowers,
and then he went and locked the bride
in the vestry safe for hours!'

ANIMAL ANTICS!

A baby camel asked its mother
'Why have we got large feet?'
'To stop us sinking deep into
the desert sand, my sweet.'

The baby said 'Around my eyes
I've got a lot of hair!'
Its mother said 'That stops the sand
from getting everywhere.'

The baby said 'Upon our backs,
why have we got three lumps?'
Its mother said 'My little one,
we camels call them humps.'

 'Sometimes we walk for days and days,
and find the desert dry,
so when we can't find water-holes
we have our own supply.'

The baby camel looked confused.
 'If what you say is true,
then what are we both doing here
each day at London Zoo?!'

A young girl on a Summer's day
was going for a walk.
She saw a frog, and was surprised
to hear the creature talk!

 'Kiss me' it said, 'and I will be
your prince!' She said 'What for?
I really think a talking frog
is worth a great deal more!'

CHILDREN SAY THE FUNNIEST THINGS!

Young Pat was only seven, but was
as helpful as she could be.
One morning she said to her parents
'I've bought you a nice cup of tea.'

She wasn't allowed to use the kettle,
but her mother didn't speak.
She took a small sip, and found it was
very lukewarm and weak.

'How did you make the tea, my dear?'
she said to her daughter Pat.
'My hot water bottle was still quite warm,
so I used the water from that!'

'We're descended from apes' young Jimmy said.
'That's right,' his mother replied.
' I just wondered' the young lad continued,
'if it was your side or Daddy's side?'

The teacher asked her children to draw
the feeding of the five thousand one day.
Only five minutes had passed before
Jimmy put his picture away.

She went to inspect his drawing,
and said in a tone of despair.
'I asked you to draw five thousand.
There's only one person there!'

The classroom erupted in laughter,
but quite unabashed, the young lad
said 'The rest got fed up and went home, Miss,
because of the long wait they'd had!'

COFFEE BREAK

A shopkeeper was in hospital
with his family round his bed.
Weakly, the old man opened his eyes.
'Is my dear wife here?' he said.

'Yes dear.' He then asked 'What about
my daughter Ruth?' She said 'I'm here.'
'What about my sons, Matthew and Thomas?'
They said 'Dad, we're both very near.'

At that the old man sat upright in bed
and said 'This nonsense must stop!
I have got a living to make.
Will someone get back to the shop?!'

'Local man wanted for half million bank robbery'
the evening newspaper read.
One man who saw it, got quite excited.
'I think I'll apply' he said!

The tailor measured him for a suit.
'We'll do it in six weeks if we can.'
'Six weeks!' the customer cried, looking grim.
'That seems a long time, my man!'

'God made the world in six days, you know.'
The tailor replied with a grin.
'That may be perfectly true, sir,
but look what a state it is in!'

The vicar and his wife went for fish and chips.
'The usual, dear, with thick sliced bread.'
At that she called out to the kitchen.
'Can you save two soles?' she said!

CHURCH CHUCKLES!

The treasurer spoke to the church and said
  'I have a piece of bad news.
The church roof is leaking quite badly
and we have to replace all the pews.'

  'I'm afraid it will cost quite a lot, friends,
but nobody need look too glum.
I have a piece of good news now.
We know how the money will come.'

  'We've worked all the finances out,
and answered each 'Why', 'When' and 'How'.
The bad news friends, is that the money
is all in your pockets right now!'

He asked 'Dad, can I borrow your car
now that I've passed my test?'
His father said 'You can, if you
do all that I suggest.'

  'Work hard at your exams, and do
the very best you can,
then get your long hair cut before
you ask me again, young man!'

The lad worked hard and got good grades,
and told his father so.
His father said 'I'm pleased with you.
Your hair's not been cut though!'

His son replied 'But Jesus and
His disciples had long hair!'
  'Yes' said his father, 'but you know
they all walked everywhere!'

SHOPPING STORIES!

While shopping in her local store
she thought a jumper nice,
but told the shop assistant
  'That's far too high a price!'

'Well madam, it's a breed of sheep
that really is quite rare.
It is a truly lovely yarn
I think beyond compare!'

The shopper wasn't too impressed.
  'I won't buy it, thank you.
It's certainly a lovely yarn.
You tell it so well, too!'

Plans for the smaller shopkeeper
have been announced today.
They say that lower counters
will help in every way!

The supermarket trolleys
in his garden were piled high.
A policeman came along the road
and asked the reason why.

The owner said 'I know when
there's a bargain to be found.
Down at the supermarket
they only cost one pound!

He said 'I finished a film last week.'
  'Do you mean you're an actor?' she cried.
  'No, I'm going to Boots the Chemist
to pick it up now' he replied!

LOVELINES!

'Could you be happy with a boy like me?
he felt tempted to ask her one day.
 'Perhaps, if I didn't see you too often'
the unfortunate lad heard her say!

 'You've advertised for a husband, I hears.
Now, are you getting on fine?'
 'Everyone answers my advert' she said
 'and tells me 'You're welcome to mine'!'

He said 'We're having Chicken Surprise
for dinner tonight, I hear.
What's the surprise?' She answered him
 'You're cooking it, my dear!'

The bridegroom asked 'Will you put up with me
for the rest of our married life?'
 'You'll be out at work for most of the time,
so of course' said his young wife!

He had a new girlfriend every week.
It's catch, attach, then despatch!
He says 'When the light of my life goes out
I just strike another match!'

 'My husband won a trip for two!'
Her friend said 'That was nice.'
 'Well, you don't know my husband.
He didn't take me, but went twice!'

She spent the whole day dressmaking and sewing,
and altering all of her hems.
She asked 'Would I look nice in something
flowing?'
Her bored husband said 'Yes, the Thames!

CHILDREN SAY THE FUNNIEST THINGS!

The teacher of the infant class
asked 'What do shepherds do?'
One little boy put up his hand
and said he thought he knew.

The teacher said 'That's good, Simon,'
but then to her surprise
he said 'We bought one yesterday.
Please Miss, shepherds make pies!'

John Lewis phoned up a customer
about a delivery.
The telephone was answered by
five year old Timothy.

The small boy seemed confused, and called
  'It's the telephone, Mummy.
She says she is John Lewis,
but it sounds like his wife to me!'

'Now Jimmy, why did you throw that cup
at your lovely little sister?'
He looked at his mother, then answered
  'Because the saucer missed her!'

Young Jonathan was only three
when he first went on a plane.
He ran around, and kept looking out
of the windows, again and again.

His other told him to sit still.
  'What are you looking for, dear?'
The little lad, quite disappointed,
said 'I thought God was up here!'

LIFE'S LIKE THAT!

He asked the waiter 'Is there rice pudding
on the menu today?'
The waiter said 'There was sir, but
I've wiped it all away!'

Ted put one foot in the bath
and then was filled with doubt.
Was he getting in the bath
or was he getting out?

He called to Tommy 'Do you know
what I am trying to do?'
Tommy said 'I'm coming up
the stairs, and I'll help you.'

But halfway up the stairs he stopped.
He didn't know if he
was going up or down the stairs,
so he called to Jim 'Help me!'

Jim said 'I'm fed up with you both.
You drive me mad each day!'
He banged the table loudly,
then the others heard him say.

  'Did you hear that noise? I may
be wrong, but I am sure
that someone's round the front or back
and knocking on our door!'

My school was strict! If you were bad
they suspended you that day,
and then, if you were really bad
they kicked the chair away!

CHURCH CHUCKLES!

The vicar said 'Do you remember
that I asked everybody to pray
as the church organ needed repairing,
so we started a fund straight away.'

'I am sure with your warm contributions
we will get to our final target.'
He pulled out a mouth organ, saying
　'We haven't done too well as yet!'

A vicar hugged his four year old.
She said 'Daddy, you're so strong!
I really think that you will be
God before very long!'

The vicar said 'Next week's collection
is for the assistant curate. Be kind,
as I appeal for your generous support
with that object in mind!'

The Bishop held a conference
for vicars to attend.
He had a quiet word with the Dean
who was his closest friend.

　'This looks a scriptural gathering'
he whispered to the Dean.
The Dean, a little unsure said
　'Keen disciples, do you mean?'

'Oh no' the Bishop answered him.
　'To me it's very clear
I'm looking at the multitude
that loafs and fishes here!'

CHILDREN SAY THE FUNNNIEST THINGS!

Young Jimmy ran down to breakfast, saying
'I am looking forward to
seeing the clever thing Dad's promised
that he is going to do!'

'What's that, dear?' Mother said absently.
'You know' young Jimmy said.
'He told us he'd eat his breakfast up,
while standing on his head!'

'He promised to do it, if Grandma
didn't soon disappear,
and now he's got to do it, Mum,
because Grandma is still here!'

'How did I eat before I was born?'
young Georgina asked her Mummy.
Her mother smiled, then answered 'Darling
I fed you in my tummy.'

Georgina thought, and then replied
'Now Mummy, you should have worried!
You know I don't like anything
that's either fried or curried!'

Young Tommy, who was only five
had coloured a whole page.
He'd done it neatly, and I said
'That's very good for your age.'

A little later I was painting
the outside of my shed.
'That's very good for your age, Grandpa.;
little Tommy brightly said!

COFFEE BREAK

Mr and Mrs Brown were resting
when they heard a knock on the door.
He said to her 'It's bound to be
our awful neighbour next door!'

'He'll be wanting to borrow something.
He's used half the things we own!'
She said 'If my scheme works, he may
very well leave us alone.'

'Whatever he wants to borrow
you only have to say
you're sorry, but you've already planned
to use it later today!'

Her husband beamed, and said 'Do you know
you have such good ideas!'
He went to the door. His neighbour asked
'Could I please borrow your shears?'

He said 'I'm really sorry, Bill,
but I'll be using them soon.
My wife and I will be gardening
the whole of the afternoon!'

His neighbour paused, and then replied
'I quite understand that, Len,
but as you won't be using them
can I borrow your golf clubs then?!'

Two old gentlemen met, and one said
'I live in the past all day.'
The other one said 'I don't blame you.
It's very much cheaper that way!'

ANIMAL ANTICS!

He told a friend 'My dog plays chess.'
His friend said 'That's so clever!'
He said 'Well yes, he wins sometimes,
but really hardly ever!'

A tortoise saw a psychiatrist
and said 'I'm terribly shy.'
 'I'll soon have you out of your shell'
was the psychiatrist's reply!

A famous hunter asked his friend
 'Have you hunted bear?'
His friend said 'When it's really hot,
I've shorts I sometimes wear!'

'My chicken lays square eggs' he said,
 'and it talks as well each day,
although 'ouch' is the only word
I've ever heard it say!'

The postman looked suspiciously
at one large dog he saw.
He didn't really feel like walking
past it to the door!

The owner of the house came out
and saw his nervous eyes.
She said 'He came from Africa.
I suppose he's quite a size!'

We're not quite sure what breed he is,
but really there again
he hasn't looked so frightening since
my husband cut his mane!'

LIFE'S LIKE THAT!

The teacher said to young Jimmy's mother
'He's the stupidest boy, without doubt!'
Jimmy's mother replied 'Excuse me, sir,
that's my son you're talking about.'

The teacher said 'Sorry, I didn't realise,'
and felt embarrassed as could be.
Jimmy's mother then said 'But nobody
could be half as sorry as me!'

He'd bought a brand new carriage clock
and spoke of it full of praise.
He told a friend 'Without winding,
it will go for fourteen days!'

'That's wonderful' his friend replied,
'but what I would like to know,
if you do decide to wind it up
then how long will it go?!'

'My, hasn't your little girl grown?'
the first witch loudly cried.
'I agree, she's certainly gruesome'
the second witch replied!

Sarah's mother tried to help
and bring her neighbours cheer.
'Go and see how old Mrs Jones is
across the road, Sarah dear.'

Sarah came back in a while
and looked fed up and glum.
'Mrs Jones was cross, and said it's none
of my business how old she is, Mum!'

CHURCH CHUCKLES!

The vicar in a small village
was invited to dinner one night.
He took a lantern out with him
as the lanes were not too bright.

He had a lovely evening out,
and he got home safe and sound.
The squire with whom he'd been to dine
next morning called around.

He said 'I've brought your lantern back.
We both had a drink or two,
and you must have taken my parrot
in its cage back home with you!'

A little girl hadn't been to church,
but one Spring morning she went.
They didn't decorate the church
each year when it was Lent.

So it was bare, and the organ
just wasn't played at all.
It all seemed rather strange to
somebody so very small!

The four year old was puzzled, and
her mother heard her say
  'It's very quiet in here, Mummy.
Why doesn't the organ play?'

  'Because it's Lent' her mother said.
  'Now be a good girl, won't you?'
The little girl whispered 'All right Mummy,
but who is it lent too?!'

LOVELINES!

She said 'I've seen a mind reader.'
Her husband replied 'That's nice,'
then added rather unkindly
  'Did the person charge you halfprice?!'

She'd married nine times, and the registrar
got quite used to seeing this bride!
  'Do you have trouble making up your mind?'
he asked. 'Yes and No' she replied!

I asked 'What happened to the couple
who met in a revolving door?'
My friend replied 'They're not going round
together anymore!'

He took his wife as a special treat
to the cinema last night.
As they settled down he asked her
  'Now can you see all right?'

She told him 'I can see just fine,'
and then he spoke again.
  'Is your seat really comfortable?'
She said 'As right as rain.'

He said 'You're really sure nobody's
blocking out your view?'
She answered 'No.' Her husband said
  'Well, can I change with you?!'

'My wife never uses make-up'
her husband was heard to say,
  'but that doesn't matter because
no one looks at her anyway!'

MEDICAL MATTERS!

A patient in the dentist's chair
had to have some dentures made.
The dentist made a mould, then said
'It's not good, I'm afraid.'

'I'm really very sorry,
but I'll have to do it twice.
I've made a bad impression.'
She said 'No, you're very nice!'

She said 'The doctor's such a funny chap.
He'll have you in stitches soon!'
He said 'I've only come for a check-up!
I'm going home this afternoon!'

'Doctor, I'm sorry to trouble you,
but my problem makes me so depressed.
What can you give me for flat feet?'
'A bicycle pump, I suggest!'

'Doctor, my hair keeps falling out!
Have you something to keep it in?'
'Hold on a minute. I know somewhere
I've got an old biscuit tin!'

One lady was so overweight
the doctor said 'It's unwise!
Please take these pills, and every day
you must do more exercise.'

'I am sure you'll feel a lot better,
and you won't be in such pain.
I hope to see much less of you
when you come again!'

MOTORING MADNESS!

'I'm working on a one man bus' he told me.
'I've just heard that I've passed the interview.
I'll drive the Number 17 from Tooting.
I have to collect the customers' fares too.'

Sadly, the first day that he took the bus out
he had a bit of trouble straight away!
It crashed into a bridge, and his inspector
listened to what the driver had to say.

He said 'I don't know much about the crash, sir,
for it caught me completely unawares.
I think just at the moment that it happened
I was upstairs in the bus, collecting fares!'

A taxi driver had been operated on
and lay semi-conscious in bed.
The doctor came by. 'He keeps putting out
his right arm,' the student nurse said.

'Don't worry' the doctor said to her.
'I'm sure that the danger has passed.
I think that he's giving us the sign
that he's turning the corner at last!'

A lady with ten small children
got on a bus one day.
'Are they yours, or is it a picnic?'
the driver was heard to say.

The lady looked really exhausted!
'I'm afraid they're all mine!' she sighed,
'and it's certainly not a picnic'
the harassed young mother replied!

CHILDREN SAY THE FUNNNIEST THINGS!

'I kissed Amanda on the bus,
Mummy,' young Derek said.
'She kissed me back, and said to me
it means that now we're wed!'

'Now you are married' his Mum said,
'you won't have time to play.
To earn some money for your wife
you'll have to work all day.'

'You'll have to move away from home
and buy one with your wife.
You'll have to leave school. It will be
a really busy life!'

Young Derek's face was falling till
it almost hit the floor!
He said 'Mummy, I've decided
I'm not married any more!'

When she saw a heavily-tattooed man,
a six year old girl named Joy
said 'I bet your mother took your felt tips
away when you were a boy!'

She took her son to the cinema,
on his birthday as a surprise,
but found the film quite frightening,
and kept on shutting her eyes.'

Her young son saw her eyes tightly closed
and told his nervous mum
    'You obviously don't like it.
I don't know why you've come!'

LIFE'S LIKE THAT!

'I'm not going down to the launderette'
they heard one lady shout.
  'A notice says 'Please remove your clothes
as soon as the light goes out!'

A stupid but tough sergeant major
told his men of a lecture that day.
  'It's on Keats, but all those who don't know
what a keat is can just stay away!'

A lady asked the railway porter
  'Shall I change on platform 3?'
The porter replied 'Well, if you must,
but don't let the passengers see!'

  'I'd like some crocodile shoes, please'
she asked in a shoe shop one day.
  How big is your crocodile, madam?
the salesgirl was tempted to say!

A tourist was shown round a village
by an elderly local guide.
  'Have you lived here all your life?' he asked.
  'Not yet, sir' the local replied!

I know someone who finds it hard
to be jolly and to laugh.
He made the effort the other day
to pose for a photograph.

He wrote to a 'Lonely Hearts Club',
and sent his picture too.
They wrote 'We're not that lonely.
We're returning it to you!'

CHURCH CHUCKLES!

The vicar's sermons were over-long,
but he went on holiday.
A visiting preacher filled the pulpit
the week he was away.

He rose to speak, but mercifully
his sermon was so brief.
The Churchwarden went up to him
and spoke with great relief!

The preacher said 'The dog chewed up
my notes, and so you see
she caused my sermon to be shorter
then it would normally be!

The Warden said 'If she has pups
could you give us a call?
We'll give one to our vicar
as a present from us all!'

A couple renewed the wedding vows
they'd made twenty years before,
and took the opportunity
to talk to the vicar once more.

 'Today has brought back such memories,
and we are so pleased we've met.
You made a comment on our wedding day
that we shall never forget!

 'You said we wouldn't remember
a single word you said that day,
and we just wanted to tell you
you were right in every way!'

CHILDREN SAY THE FUNNIEST THINGS!

Young Jimmy's mother said one day
'Can you be a help to me?
If you will tidy your bedroom up
I'll give you 50p.'

Young Jimmy studied all the mess
he saw as he looked around,
then told her 'If you do it, Mum,
I'll give you a whole pound!'

'Jimmy, your geography report
says that you must listen more!'
'Dad, he keeps talking about places
that I've never heard of before!'

'That essay you wrote, is really quite good
for someone your age, my lad.'
How good is it, teacher?' young Jimmy asked,
for someone the age of my Dad?!'

'My sister can spell her name backwards,
and she is only five!'
'How clever!' the teacher said ''What's her name?'
'Anna' said her brother Clive!

Two boys were talking outside a posh school.
'I told my chauffeur' said Bob,
'to take his peaked cap off in case
the boys thought that I was a snob!'

'That's really quite a coincidence'
replied the other posh lad.
'I told mine to keep his on in case
the boys thought that he was my Dad!'

COFFEE BREAK

'My insurance man's asking far too much
for the premium' he said.
'Last week he asked five times for it,
and five times I shook my head!'

A man returned the purse she'd lost
when it fell out of her coat.
She checked it, then she said to him
'I had a twenty pound note.'

'Now I have got four five pound notes.
That's really very strange!'
The man said 'If there is a reward
I thought you might need some change!'

He had an interview for a job
and told them This job sounds fine.
The trouble is, my last employment
was absolutely divine!'

'I got paid more, had bonuses
with paid overtime each day.
I had a generous travel allowance
and holidays with pay.

'I had a very cheap mortgage
and an excellent pension scheme.
It was the kind of job that folk
would think was just a dream!'

He said 'Whatever made you leave?
You seem a sensible bloke.'
The man replied 'I had to leave
because the firm went broke!'

ANIMAL ANTICS!

'Now, why do dogs scratch themselves?'
I was asked by my cousin Fred.
'Because they're the only ones who know
where they are itching' he said!

Two slugs were walking out one day
when two snails passed them by.
'These posh folk in their caravans!'
said one slug with an envious eye!

Noah's sons were fishing from the Ark.
Noah said 'Whatever you do,
don't use the worms we brought along.
We've only got the two!'

'It's really windy here!' they heard
the farmer's young son say.
'One of my father's chickens laid
the same egg three times today!'

In a large Safari Park
on a lovely warm Summer's day
a family of lions around
a clump of trees sleepily lay.

A car packed full of tourists
drove very slowly by,
and father lion, ever alert
opened a watchful eye.

He said to all his family
'I really do despair!
It seems a shame on such a day
to be caged up in there!'

LOVELINES!

He told a friend 'For thirty years
I've tried to love my wife.
At least I've learned to understand
the simpler things in life!'

'They say I have an infectious laugh'
she said to her husband-to-be.
  'In that case' he replied 'I hope
that you don't laugh too near me!'

'I was cut out to be a genius'
her husband boasted one day.
  'Pity the pieces don't fit properly'
his wife was tempted to say!

His friend asked him 'Does your wife use
a mud pack to look her best?'
  'It works for a few days till the mud
falls off' he said in jest!

He told his wife 'I do love being
tickled under the chin.'
His wife answered 'Tell me which one,
and then I can begin!'

He found out that she was a nurse.
  'I wish you could nurse me!'
She said 'I don't think that is likely as
I work in Maternity!'

She said 'I'm suffering from bad breath,
but I'm hoping it will pass away,
because I am taking my husband
to visit the dentist today!

CHURCH CHUCKLES!

Class 4 did their Nativity play
at Christmas time last year.
The teacher chose Joseph, then told him
'Your costume's too small, I fear.'

'Still, you can be the innkeeper.
That part's important too.
The little lad was quite upset
but bravely saw it through.

The play began. Mary and Joseph
arrived at Bethlehem.
'May we come in please?' Joseph asked.
The innkeeper looked at them.

He suddenly felt so annoyed,
and forgetting what he should say
he said to Mary 'You can come in,
but Joseph can go away!'

Each week our congregation
all sit glued to their chairs.
We find that is the only way
the vicar can keep them there!'

Each time the devil was mentioned
an old man would bow his head.
The vicar was rather curious
and thought he'd speak to old Ted.

'It doesn't seem right' said the vicar.
Old Ted replied 'That may be so,
but a bit of politeness costs nothing,
and vicar, you just never know!'

SPORTING STORIES!

The golfer asked 'Have you packed all
my stuff in the car, my dear?'
She answered 'Yes, your clubs, and maps
and emergency rations are here!'

The judge said 'Prisoner at the bar,
I find you 'Not Guilty.
You didn't steal those golf clubs,
and I'm going to set you free.'

The prisoner said 'Thank you, my Lord.
I'm the happiest of men!'
Your Honour, does that mean that I
can keep the golf clubs then?!'

Two golfers had a game, and were
enjoying it a lot,
until one took a lengthy time
to work out his next shot.

His partner said 'Please hurry up.
You're holding up the play!'
The other golfer said 'My wife
has come to watch today.'

She's standing at the clubhouse
behind the eighteenth tee,
and I want this to be the best
long drive you'll ever see!'

The first man said 'Well, have a go,
but I think it's quite clear.
You haven't got a chance at all
of hitting her from here!'

CHILDREN SAY THE FUNNIEST THINGS!

Jimmy's father read his school report
and said 'It's awful Son!
I think of all the reports you've had
this is the very worse one!'

'I knew you wouldn't like it.
The teacher is to blame.
I told her not to send it,
but she insisted, just the same!'

Jimmy's teacher got so fed up
with his fooling about each day
that she wrote a letter of complaint.
His father read it straight away.

'Now what's this all about, my lad?
She says that she's going to call,
because she finds it impossible
to teach you anything at all!'

Jimmy was never lost for words,
and replied quite cheerfully
  'If she can't teach me anything
she can't be much good, can she?!'

Jimmy said 'The teacher says I'm as smart
as the boy who sits next to me!
The trouble is, he added that we're both
as stupid as could be!'

Young Jimmy answered the phone one day,
and heard 'long distance from Japan.'
Jimmy said that he knew that,
and hung up on the man!

LIFE'S LIKE THAT!

A lady phoned her grocer up
to angrily complain.
   'My boy came for three pounds of nuts.
We've been short changed again.

She asked him if his scales were right.
He said 'I'm really sure,
but did you check your son to see
how much he weighted before?!'

A man went down to a pub each night
and drank three pints of beer.
The landlord liked the man, and said
   'Thankyou for coming here.'

He asked him why he had three points
and never less or more.
He said he had two brothers whom
he hardly ever saw.

He said' We've made a promsie that
whatever else we do,
we'll drink three pints each day, so we
can toast the other two!'

Six months went by, and then he ordered
just two pints one night.
The worried landlord asked him if
his brothers were all right.

   'Oh yes, the man replied at once,
and then went on to say
   'but I have just decided to
stop drinking from today!

MEDICAL MATTERS

A lecturer in a medical school
was showing his students X-rays.
He said 'Without some form of treatment
this patient will limp always.'

He turned to a young man, and asked him
 'Now my good man, what would you do?'
The young trainee doctor said 'Well sir,
I'm certain that I would limp too!'

 'My wife didn't have enough sleeping tablets!'
her husband was heard to complain.
The doctor said 'Why?' The husband replied
 'She's just woken up again!'

She asked 'Do you take out teeth painlessly?'
not wishing to come to harm.
The dentist replied 'Not always, madam.
Last week I dislocated my arm!'

The doctor came out of his surgery
at the end of his afternoon shift.
He saw Mrs Thompson was walking,
so he gave the old lady a lift.

 'I have not seen you round here for ages!
I'm still practising here' he said.
Mrs Thompson said 'Doctor, I've decided
I'll come back when you're perfect, instead!'

A lad went into a chemist's shop
and requested a box of pills.
 'Antibilious?' the chemist asked helpfully.
 'No, it's my uncle who is ill!'

COFFEE BREAK

The Duke and Duchess had hired a new maid
to work on their family estate.
  'Remember' the Duchess said haughtily,
'that we always have breakfast at eight!'

The maid nodded her head in agreement,
and replied 'Yes, that seems quite okay.
If I'm still asleep, just start without me.
I don't eat much breakfast, anyway!'

A politician had a large audience.
  'I'm delighted to see this dense crowd.'
  'Don't be too delighted. We're not all dense'
one young man shouted out loud!

  'Mr Jones, you're a father!' the nurse said.
  'Is it a boy, nurse?' he cried.
She tried to break the news gently.
  'The one in the middle is' she replied!

The judge said 'For your many crimes
you're imprisoned for twenty years!
The defendant, who was eighty four
could not believe his ears.

  'I'll never live to do all that'
replied the elderly man.
  'Don't get upset' the judge told him.
  'Just do as much as you can!'

His friend, who was rather a miser
was stripping wallpaper one day.
He asked him 'Are you decorating?'
He replied 'No, I'm moving away!'

CHURCH CHUCKLES!

A new vicar arrived in the parish,
and folk were quite pleased when he came.
The one problem was that his sermons
all sounded exactly the same!

This went on for quite a few weeks till
someone plucked up the courage to say
 'I just wondered vicar, if your sermon
was the same as you preached last Sunday?'

The vicar smiled, then said 'I wondered
when someone would question as you are.
To be perfectly honest, I've now preached
the same sermon eight times so far!'

 'I've many more sermons prepared, friend,
but that would be jumping the gun.
I'm still waiting for those that I preach to
to act on the very first one!'

 'Jonah spent three days in the big fish
singing and practising his scales.'
When they asked young Hugh why he said that,
he said 'Everybody sings in Wales!'

The vicar went down to the infant school
to speak to the children one day.
He wanted to talk about Jesus
and see what they all had to say.

He asked 'What happened on Christmas Day?'
and one little girl sitting there
put up her hand and said innocently
 'My Daddy was sick on the stairs!'

LOVELINES!

'Can I carry your baggage?' a husband was asked
at a terribly posh hotel.
The husband replied 'My wife is perfectly
able to walk quite well!'

She went to the hotel to book a room.
'Single?' the receptionist said.
The lady told her 'At the moment,
but I am engaged to be wed!'

She said 'I've been asked to get married
hundreds of times you know!'
She added 'It's my parents who ask me,
because they both want me to go!'

'You're looking much better' the doctor said.
'Now, how's that terrible pain?'
'Well, actually doctor' the patient replied
'she's gone to her mother's again!'

He asked 'Do you find life boring?'
She answered with some regret
'Well, no, I never used to,
but that was before we met!'

'They say that ignorance is bliss'
a husband told his wife.
She said to him 'well you should have
a very happy life!'

'My husband wants to work badly'
she told a friend one day.
'He works so badly though, no one
is ever willing to pay!'

CHILDREN SAY THE FUNNIEST THINGS!

Jimmy's father said 'I hear that in maths
you came bottom out of ten!'
He said 'My friend came bottom of twenty,
so I didn't do so bad, then!'

Two small boys were in a modern art gallery
and young Jimmy said to Mick,
'Before they say we did it
we had better get out quick!'

'I don't deserve zero for my homework'
young Jimmy cried in distress!
The teacher said 'I know you don't,
but I can't give you any less!'

'Where did you get that language from?'
'William Shakespeare', young Jimmy said.
'Well, you'd better stop going round with him.
Choose another friend, instead!'

'Does anyone know what a goose eats?'
Young Jimmy boldly replied.
'I think that it eats gooseberries, Sir!'
His poor school teacher sighed!

'I'd like to paint the garage door'
said helpful little John.
His father said 'That's kind of you.
You must put two coats on.'

Later that afternoon he found
the garage painted bright blue,
and John wearing a jacket and raincoat
saying 'Dad, you told me to!'

ANIMAL ANTICS!

A penguin went into a pub and asked
  'Has my friend been in today?'
  'Can you tell me what he looked like?'
he heard the landlord say!

Two lions were doing their shopping.
One said to the other 'My dear,
each time we come, have you noticed
how peaceful and quiet it is here?!'

A dears old lady called at a shop
saying 'Have you some wool I can buy?
My dog gets very cold, and I think I'd like
to knit him a sweater, that's why.

The saleswoman said 'Certainly my dear.
Can you tell me your dog's size?
Better still can you bring him in?'
She said, 'No, it's to be a surprise!'

Jimmy saw a bull in Farmer Giles' field.
  'Is that bull safe?' he cried.
  'I'd say that he's a whole lot safer
than you' Farmer Giles replied!

'Why do mother kangaroos
hate rainy days?' asked Tim.
  'Because their children have to play
inside' I answered him!

  'Is your dog fond of children?'
Johnny nervously asked a man.
  'Well yes he is, but he'd rather have
a biscuit when he can!'

LIFE'S LIKE THAT!

A man was looking for aftershave
in a large superstore one day.
He asked an assistant who said 'I'll see,'
and then just wandered away!

Ten minutes later she hadn't come back,
so he asked someone else in the store.
 'I'll see' he said, then he just went off,
and didn't come back anymore!

He went to the manager's office
and he said 'I am here to complain'
I want to know where the aftershave is.'
The manager said 'I'll see' again!

He then stormed out of the office,
feeling as cross as could be,
till he suddenly noticed the aftershave
where they said, in Aisle C!

They make the smallest computers
that people have yet seen.
The boss told me that business was
the best it had ever been.

He said 'If we continue
to progress and improve,
we'll need much smaller premises
and so we'll have to move!'

 'Did you meet your son at the airport?'
he asked his neighbour's wife.
She answered 'Well, to tell the truth
I've known him all his life!'

COFFEE BREAK

They asked a lady asked one hundred and two
what worries she had. She said 'None.
Not since I found an old peoples' home
to take in my eldest son!'

She'd always found it hard to show
her feelings through the years,
and so she thought she'd buy a book
to give her fresh ideas.

She bought a book marked 'How to Hug,'
but later on she saw
it was one reference volume from
a set of twenty four!

Two men were jailed on the same day,
and then found out as well
the prison warders had arranged
for them to share a cell.

  'How long will be you be here?' one asked.
  'Ten years' the other said.
  'I've got twenty, so you had better
have the nearest bed!'

A man drove his pet goldfish
to the fish shop in his car.
He marked up to the counter
with the goldfish in a jar.

  'Have you got a fishcake
for my precious little pet?
You see,. today's his birthday
and I'm not one to forget!'

CHURCH CHUCKLES!

A vicar was leaving his parish
where he'd lived for many a day.
When he preached his final sermon
he had so many things to say.

'It is my proud boast' said the vicar,
'and a source of contentment to me
that I shall be shortly preparing
to depart without one enemy!'

One brave lady tackled the vicar
at his farewell tea, held in the hall.
She asked him 'Why are you so certain?'
He replied 'I have buried them all!'

One parishioner will always choose
to grumble or to groan.
'The vicar has three basic faults'
has become his latest moan!

'He reads his sermons every week,
and very badly, I say,
and lastly I don't think they are
worth reading, anyway!'

'Lord, give them all pure hearts'
the vicar preached one day,
'and give them all clean hearts,
we earnestly do pray.'

The vicar really meant well,
but quite forgetting his text,
carried away he cried out
'Give them all sweet hearts' next!'

CHILDREN SAY THE FUNNIEST THINGS!

'Now, what do ghosts like in their coffee?'
young Jimmy asked me today,
then said 'Evaporated milk!' before
he chuckled, and ran away!

'Come away from that biscuit tin, Jimmy
or we'll certainly have a row!
How many more times must I tell you?'
'None, Mum. It's empty now!'

'Now, have you read Dickens, Claire?'
'No, Miss,' the little girl said.
'Have you read Shakespeare?' 'No, Miss.'
'Well then Claire, what have you read?'

After she'd thought for a moment
'I know, Miss' answered young Claire.
'So what have you read then, my dear?'
'Teacher' she said 'I've read hair!'

'Please write 'I must not forget my sports kit'
one hundred times, now Claire.;
Claire said 'I only forgot it once!
That seems a bit unfair!'

'Jimmy, one of your essays is very good,
and the other is quite bad!'
'Yes sir, I find that my Mum
does much better than my Dad!'

'Now, how many make a dozen?'
'12', said little Sue.
'How many make a million?'
'My Dad says, very few!'

LIFE'S LIKE THAT!

My neighbour has the final word,
no matter what I do!
I said to her 'We're moving soon.
I thought I would tell you.'

'Yes, we have bought a brand new home
in a much nicer place.'
'That's nice for you' my neighbour said,
with a smile upon her face.

'We too will soon be living in
a better area, dear.'
I asked 'Why, are you moving too?'
'Oh no, we're staying here!'

'Except for two things' Susan's mother was told
'her dancing would be so neat.';
Unfortunately for Susan, the teacher
was talking about her feet!

A teacher took her children to
an old folks home one day.
She told them all to circulate,
and simply chat away.

'This lady's nearly ninety nine!'
two little girls were told.
They both sat by her chair, and asked
her 'Are you really old?'

She had a twinkle in her eye,
and said to them 'My dears,
no I'm not old, but I've been young
for very many years!'

COFFEE BREAK

Three absent minded men were chatting,
waiting for a train,
but luckily they heard the guard
blow once, and then again.

He shouted 'Take your seats!' and so
they hurried to get on.
Two caught the train, but one was left
and cried 'My train has gone!'

A passing porter heard his cry
and said 'Don't be too sad.
At least your friends have both got on,
so things are not too bad.'

The absent minded man looked up
and said with a deep sigh
  'I booked this train to go abroad.
They came to say 'Goodbye'!'

A lady had been looking at
some suitcases one day.
She spent so long, the sales assistant
wished she'd go away!

The lady carried on, and then
she turned round in the end
and said 'I've not come here to buy.
I'm looking for a friend.;

The sales assistant wearily
said 'If it helps at all
I'll help you check our luggage out.
Is your friend very small?!'

LOVELINES!

'You know that cake I made this morning.
There's a burglar eating a piece!'
Her husband said 'Now, shall I phone
the ambulance or the police?!'

She told her husband 'I've changed my mind.'
He answered 'About time too.
I hope that you find the new one
will work much better for you!'

She asked her husband 'If I'm run down,
what exactly should I do?'
Her husband said 'I'd take the number
of the car if I was you!'

She said 'If you were my husband
I'd poison your coffee today!'
He answered 'If you were my wife
I'd drink it all straight away!'

She asked him 'Will you love me
when I'm old and wrinkly too?'
He looked at her and nodded
''My dear, you know I do!'

He was a portrait painter
and he chose to paint his wife.
When he had finished it 'he said
'I think that's true to life.'

She said 'It does look better
when you stand further away.'
'I said that it was just like you'
she heard her husband say!

CHURCH CHUCKLES!

A man called at the Pearly Gates one day.
The angel said 'We're not expecting you!'
When he said 'I was a scrap metal merchant'
the angel said 'I'll have to check it through.'

The angel checked, and then came back to find
there wasn't anybody there to tell.
The scrap metal merchant had vanished without
trace.
What was worse, the Pearly Gates had gone as
well.

There is a notice in our church
about which I must tell.
'Don't let worry kill you.
The church can help as well!'

A vicar was sent a bottle
of cherries in brandy one day.
He wrote out a note of gratitude
for the gift that had come his way.

'Although I don't care much for cherries,
the present was thoughtfully meant,
and I did appreciate the spirit
in which the cherries were sent!'

'Now, why did the Children of Israel
make a Golden Calf long ago?'
A little boy sitting at the back
said 'Please Miss, I think I know.'

'Now Jeremy, that is very good.
Please give me the answer now.'
'Miss, was it because they didn't have
enough gold to make a cow?!'

MEDICAL MATTERS!

At three o'clock in the morning
the doctor gave a loud groan.
He stumbled downstairs, just in time
to answer the telephone!

'I'm sorry to trouble you, doctor'
he heard the caller say.
'That's quite all right. I had to get up
to answer it, anyway!'

'I'm becoming invisible, Doctor!'
a patient cried in despair.
The doctor didn't help by saying
'I can see that you're not all there!'

'Doctor, I think I need glasses.'
He said 'You certainly do!
This has been a fish and chip shop
for at least the last year or two!'

He said 'Doctor, I keep eating apples.
I just can't eat one more!'
The doctor said 'I'll examine you.
We'll soon get to the core!'

'Doctor, you've taken my tonsils and adenoids,
gall bladder and varicose veins.
You've also taken my appendix out,
but I get all these aches and pains!'

'I don't think I'm one for complaining,
but Doctor, what can you do?'
The doctor thought for a moment, then said
'That's quite enough out of you!'

CHILDREN SAY THE FUNNIEST THINGS!

'Now, how was your first day at school?'
'I've not had my present' said Fred!
'The teacher showed me to a chair.
'Sit there for the present' she said!

'Now Jimmy, you've been fighting again.
I'm really cross with you!
You have to learn to give and take
in everything you do.'

'Well Dad, I did exactly that
said Jimmy, looking vexed.
'I gave that Tommy a black eye,
and took his apple next!'

'Each night when I am wide awake,
my Mum puts me to bed,
and she gets me up each morning
when I'm really sleepy' she said!

'You must control your temper, Jimmy!
You know it isn't right.
Each time you come back home from school
you've been in another fight!'

She said 'I told you to count to ten.'
'But Mum, I came off worst!
Tommy's Mum tells him to count to five
and so he hit me first!'

'What is the plural of mouse?'
'Mice', replied little Lee.
'What is the plural of baby?'
'Twins,' he called out with glee!

ANIMAL ANTICS!

A man took his pet dog to a church
and asked 'Can we both come inside?'
The vicar said 'Well, just this once.
If you sit at the back he can hide.'

The owner was grateful, and sat at the back.
The service began very soon.
His pet dog stood up on the pew and sang
each hymn completely in tune!

His singing brought tears to the eyes
of all the dear folk who were there.
He even knelt down with his master
and shut his eyes for every prayer!

His singing was heard by the vicar
who spoke to the man at the end.
'I wanted to tell you your lovely pet dog
has a beautiful voice, my friend!'

'I think with some training, you know
one day he can go very far.
In my opinion he has the voice
to become an opera star!'

The owner was moved by the vicar's remarks
and turned to his dog and said
'Did you hear that? Do you still want to be
a taxi driver instead?!'

A single herring can have a million
babies!' the teacher told Sue.
She said 'I think the married ones
must have even more, don't you?!'

LIFE'S LIKE THAT!

Now little Petal Tuckett
put her head inside a bucket,
then thought she'd wear it every single day.
Folk would point and hail her
saying 'My, you're looking 'paler.'
But Petal carried on her own sweet way.

They called out 'Look at Petal
for she's into heavy metal!'
and people felt she'd really flipped her lid.
While some folk mocked and scorned her
others gently warned her,
but Petal seemed content with all she did.

Young Petal clanged and clattered,
and cats and dogs all scattered
every time she walked along the road.
Such large crowds started queuing
to see what she was doing
and traffic piled up as the drivers slowed.

One day with no real warning
a hoot of wasps came swarming,
and one by one the crowd all felt their sting
It affected them quite sorely,
and most of them were poorly
but clever Petal never felt a thing!

A large lady got on a bus.
It was crowded and she made a fuss.
  'Who will give up his seat?'
Three men got to their feet
and said with a smile 'All of us!'

CHURCH CHUCKLES!

The chapel had an old fashioned stove
on which a kettle stood.
It whistled as the preacher finished,
as all good kettles should!

The visiting preacher told the steward
  'That's such a good idea.'
He said 'We only half fill it
for some that we get here!'

The vicar said 'Our new missionary
is coming to speak on Sunday.
Is there anybody here who is prepared
to have him for lunch on Monday?!'

'The choir will murder the anthem.
The organist will drown the choir,
and we have a canon in the pulpit,
but be brave and come for an hour!'

The Church Secretary gave the notices
  'If you all check up, you'll find
one lady at last week's social
must have left her watch behind.'

'If she can see me afterwards
she can have it straight away.
We'll sing another hymn before
the vicar comes to pray.'

  'Now, really quite appropriately
the next hymn is going to be
  'Lord her watch Thy church is keeping.'
Hymn Number 73!'

COFFEE BREAK

For ten years I'd wanted a new three piece suite,
and finally bought it this year.
How well I remember the moment when
the delivery man bought it here!

I opened the door in excitement.
 'I've been waiting for ten years!' I cried.
 'Don't blame me sir, for I only received
your order today' he replied!

A drunk approached a street lamp
and got out his door key.
He was trying to fit it in the lamp
when a policeman happened to see.

 'I don't think anyone's at home!'
said the policeman, with a grin.
 'But officer, the upstairs light
is on. Somebody must be in!'

The cannibal said to the clown 'You know
I won't eat you for love or money,
because I tried a clown once before
and he tasted very funny!'

A friend of mine took some exams
and felt so tense and stressed.
She said 'I think I'm going to fail
every single test.'

 'Think positively' I replied,
 'and then the job's half done.'
 'All right' she said, and then told me
 'I will fail every one!'

CHILDREN SAY THE FUNNIEST THINGS!

'Christmas was coming, and she asked her class
to draw the Nativity scene.
For a while there was glorious silence,
and even young Jimmy seemed keen!

'Put down your pens' she said after an hour,
and started to check them all out.
When she got to Jimmy, at first she looked pleased
and then her face creased up with doubt.

'You've drawn it quite well' she told the young lad,
but what in the corner is this?'
'Oh that' said Jimmy 'is quite obvious.
'I've put in their television, Miss!'

A boy had started infant school.
She asked 'How old are you?'
He looked at her indignantly!
'I'm not old. I'm nearly new!'

'Is your cold better?' I asked young Jimmy
yesterday afternoon.
He replied 'I've got a very bad head,
but I hope to shake it off soon!'

Young Jimmy was tearing his homework up,
and scattering it around!
His teacher asked 'What are you doing,
littering our playground?'

'It's to keep away the elephants,'
Jimmy said quite cheekily.
'But Jimmy, there are no elephants.'
'Then it works, Miss, don't you agree?!'

CHURCH CHUCKLES!

'In your sermon this morning, vicar
you had a point to make.
You said it was wrong to profit
from someone else's mistake.'

.'I just wanted to make quite sure
that you believe that's true.'
The vicar nodded, replying
'My friend, I most certainly do!'

'You conducted the marriage service
on the day that we were wed.
I thought you might consider refunding
your fees' the husband said!

'Lord, give us this day'
a little boy said
'our own fresh, protein packed,
wholemeal daily bread!'

'Friends, our vicar is leaving today,
and please don't think this odd,
but for our next hymn we shall sing
'Now thank we all our God!'

The teacher was talking of Noah's Ark,
and her question caught them unawares!
'Now, who were the only creatures
not to go in the ark in pairs?'

Young Jimmy as usual was eager
to call out 'I think I know this.
I'm sure that you mean the two maggots,
for they went in an apple, Miss!'

LOVELINES!

Their marriage wasn't going well,
and so they went along
to see a marriage counsellor
to find out what was wrong.

The counsellor asked questions, then
he hugged and kissed the wife.
He told the husband 'This is what
she needs throughout her life!'

'If this could happen just three times
a week, may I suggest
the matter will soon solve itself
and work out for the best!'

The husband said 'I thank you, sir
for knowing what to do.
Just tell me which three days I have
to bring her in to you!'

'Our little boy has done so well!'
the father said with glee
   'He's really so intelligent.
He gets it all from me.'

'Yes I agree' his wife replied.
'Our boy has turned out fine.
I'm sure his brains have come from you
because I've still got mine!'

A hen pecked man phoned the doctor to say
   'My wife's dislocated her jaw.
Can you come over to see her, please,
but leave it a few weeks or more!'

CHILDRENS PRAYERS

'I've read Your book, the Bible'
young Jeremy said, then unsure
he added 'Dear God, can You tell me,
did You ever write any more?!'

'Dear God' young Timmy prayed one night,
'I've been good, as You can see.
I've done my part of the deal, so where's
the bike You promised me?!'

'Please make my sister prettier God,'
they heard their young son call.
'Then she can marry, and move out, as
my bedroom's far too small!'

'Dear God, it has rained for several days
and nights' young Rachel cried.
'My Dad has said we'll need an Ark
to get around outside!'

'I'm asking You if You will stop
the rain immediately.
The Ark could only take two cats,
and You know we've got three!'

Young Fred was quite an ambitious child,
and filled with good intent.
He wanted to be an inventor, and prayed
'God, please show me what to invent!'

Mark prayed 'The people next to us
keep arguing constantly.
I think only good friends should marry.
Dear God, do You agree?!'

LIFE'S LIKE THAT!

They won a real fortune on
the lottery this year.
Her husband said 'Now what about
the begging letters, dear?'

His wife replied 'We mustn't change
the habits that we've got.
We'll keep on sending them, although
we won't send such a lot!'

I met her at the frozen meats.
    'You're very nice' I told her.
She smiled at me, and that made me
become a little bolder.

I said to her 'We could go out
before we get much older.'
Alas, I'd judged things wrong because
she gave me the cold shoulder!

A person I know swallows swords.
I met him last week and he said
    'My doctor's put me on a diet,
and I have pins and needles instead!'

Because their boat had overturned
they radioed for aid.
The operator said 'Capsize?
We're here. Don't be afraid.'

There was a pause, then someone called
    'Come quick! We're treading water.
I don't know how my cap size helps,
but it's seven and one quarter!'

MEDICAL MATTERS!

'I have an inferiority complex.
Doctor, can you please help me out?'
The doctor said 'You really are
inferior, of that there's no doubt!'

'Doctor, I think that I'm a clock!
Can you help me? Please be quick.'
The doctor said 'I'll examine you
and find out what makes you tick!'

'Doctor, I've got tonsillitis'
said the patient, looking grim.
'I'll check to see which leg it's in'
the student doctor told him!

'Doctor, there's something wrong with my stomach!'
The doctor said 'Well, my good lad,
if you button your jacket as best as you can
it won't look quite so bad!'

'Our Jimmy won't be at school today.
He's managed to break a thumb!'
'Tell him to get well' said the teacher.
'It was mine' said Jimmy's mum!

'My son has swallowed some gunpowder!'
The doctor said 'I see.
Now, can I ask you just one thing?
Please don't point him at me!'

Doctors wear masks for operations,
so if there is ever a hitch
nobody will be able to find
out which doctor is which!'

COFFEE BREAK

'What do you do?' he asked a young lady,
plucking up courage to chat.
'I'm an infant teacher' she replied.
He said 'I thought you were older than that!'

Young Jimmy's mother said one day
 'Shall I take him to the zoo?'
Her husband said 'If they want him,
let them collect him too!'

The teacher thinks Jimmy's a wonder child
She gave his mother a ring
and told her she wonders whether
he'll ever learn anything!

 'Can you give me a room and a bath?'
the porter was asked by a guess.
The porter said 'Yes, we can give you a room,
but our guests bath themselves, we suggest!'

A very large lady boarded a bus
and noticed that each seat was taken.
She called 'Is there a gentleman here?'
One small man was visibly shaken!

He got to his feet, and answering, said
 'It won't be the whole solution,
but if I can, madam, I'd like to make
 a very small contribution!'

A tramp knocked on a lady's door
and asked for a slice of bread.
 'I don't feed tramps' she said to him.
 'I can feed myself' he said!

CHILDREN SAY THE FUNNIEST THINGS!

Young Jimmy and his mother
went to a large local store.
It was December, and Father Christmas
was busily working once more.

'What would you like?' Father Christmas asked.
'A football and roller skates too.'
Father Christmas replied 'I'll do all I can
to get these presents to you.'

Next week they went to another store.
Father Christmas again saw him.
He asked the same question, and got
the same answer of course from young Jim.

'And are you going to be a good boy?'
Father Christmas decided to add.
That didn't go down too well at all
with a rather mischievous young lad!

He turned to his mother, and told her
'I think this is rather unfair.
Can we go back to the other store?
I didn't make promises there!'

A little boy went up to a man
and asked 'Have you lost a pound?'
The man replied 'I think I have,'
feeling his pockets and looking around.

'Have you found one?' he asked the boy.
'No' he replied straight away.
'I'm finding out how many are lost,
and yours makes fifty four today!'

ANIMAL ANTICS!

A man went into a public house
and saw a large dog lying there.
The landlord said 'He's the best rat catcher
you'll find for miles anywhere!'

Just at that moment they saw a rat
calmly strolling across the floor!
The dog lazily opened one eye, and then
he went back to sleep once more!

The customer said 'I'm not impressed.
The landlord said 'That may be so,
but when a strange rat comes into the bar
you just watch this fellow go!'

'I've bought my mother-in-law a jaguar.'
'You don't like her, and you've bought a car?!'
'It's not a car. I know what I'm doing.
It's bitten her three times so far!'

She boarded a bus, and was holding a duck!
The bus driver gave her a stare,
then after a moment he chose to say
   'That's a funny pig you have got there!'

She looked at him in some confusion,
then thinking that he must be dim
   'It's actually not a pig, young man,
but a duck!' the lady told him.

He said 'Madam, I know what a duck is
just as all my passengers do.
To be perfectly honest, it was the duck
that I was just talking to!'

THE FACTS OF LIFE!

Tommy came back home from school
saying 'Mum, can you help me?
We all have to write an essay
on how life begins, you see.'

'So how exactly was I born?'
Mum, not knowing what to say
answered 'Tommy, you were found under
a gooseberry bush one day!'

'What about Dad?' her young son asked.
'Yes Tommy, I'm telling you
that once upon a time he was found
under a gooseberry bush too!'

Young Tommy said suspiciously
'And was Grandad there as well?'
His Mum said 'Yes,' and Tommy said
'What a story I have to tell!'

He did the homework he was given.
After a week had passed
he told his mother his essay
had been marked by the teacher at last.

He said 'After you talked to me
I sat and wrote down how
we haven't had a normal birth
for three generations now!'

'The teacher said she sympathised
and really felt quite sad.
I'm to say how sorry she is
for all the trouble we've had!'

OH MR PORTER!

A man boarded a train one day
and said 'I'm going to Crewe.'
A passenger who heard him, said
 'I have bad news for you.'

'We're going past Crewe station,
but the train's not stopping there!'
 'I've got an urgent meeting!' said
the poor man in despair.

The passenger said 'There's still hope.
I've got a good idea.
I'll open up the door for you
as soon as we get near.'

 'Then I will dangle you outside,
for I am very strong.
Touch down at first, then let your legs
slow as you run along!'

He seemed a little dubious
but said 'I think I'll try.'
They got to Crewe, and out he popped,
and how those legs did fly!

He slowed, just at the platform end.
The guard opened his door,
and pulled the poor man in until
he lay upon the floor!

 'You're very lucky,' said the guard.
 'You ran so very fast
that I felt sorry, and the next
train's not till twenty past!'
